Praise For
What Kids REALLY Want to Ask

"The key to positive development among young people is high quantities of high quality time with their parents. This book gives parents and their children the knowledge and skills for engaging in warm, rich, and mutually beneficial relationships. It will be a vital resource for families navigating the early years of adolescence."—Richard M. Lerner, PhD, Director, Institute for Applied Research in Youth Development, Eliot-Pearson Department of Child Development, Tufts University

"This hands-on tool is innovative, refreshing, and practical. I love its creative approach to enhancing communication and parent-teen sharing! This unique tool is based on young teens' favorite activity: watching movies. And it guides parents and teens to use the movies as conversation-starters. Intelligent, respectful, and innovative, this is something all parents of young teens can use!"—Sue Blaney, author of *Please Stop the Rollercoaster* and speaker/consultant, ChangeWorks Publishing and Consulting

"With screen time for U.S. kids averaging over 40 hours per week, this book offers parents a way to turn some of that time into meaningful family time. Richardson and Pevec offer fun and enriching ways to share movies while deepening connections. If you're tired of getting little response when trying to converse with your middle schooler, you need this book!"—Judy Galbraith, author of *When Gifted Kids Don't Have All the Answers*

"*What Kids REALLY Want to Ask* provides an ingenious, fun, and effective way for parents and young people to connect. And it takes exactly this connection for adult wisdom to flow to kids—and for kids to offer their insights to parents. I really like this book. I enthusiastically recommend it."—Dr. Peter Benson, President and CEO, Search Institute, Minneapolis, MN

"The period right before kids hit adolescence is a time when it's critical for parents to stay in touch with their rapidly changing offspring. This book offers an intriguing, novel, and nonthreatening approach for getting parents and kids energetically involved with each other."—Thomas W. Phelan, PhD, author of *1-2-3 Magic: Effective Discipline for Children 2–12*

"Rhonda Richardson and Margaret Pevec have done parents a great favor. First they found the best movies for parents to watch with their kids. Then they provide a ton of ideas to use the flicks as ways to connect with those elusive pre-teens. This is a fun and practical resource for all parents who want to communicate with kids about important things and keep those relationships growing."—David Walsh, PhD, author of *Why Do They Act That Way? A Survival Guide to the Adolescent Brain for You and Your Teen*

What Kids
REALLY
Want to Ask

Using Movies to Start Meaningful Conversations

A Guidebook for Parents and Children Ages 10–14

RHONDA A. RICHARDSON, PHD

A. MARGARET PEVEC, MA

VanderWyk & Burnham

Published by VanderWyk & Burnham
P.O. Box 2789, Acton, Massachusetts 01720

www.VandB.com

This book is available for quantity purchases. For information on bulk discounts, call 800-789-7916, write to Special Sales at the above address, or send an e-mail to info@VandB.com.

Library of Congress Cataloging-in-Publication Data

Richardson, Rhonda A.
   What kids really want to ask : using movies to start meaningful conversations : a guidebook for parents and children ages 10-14 / Rhonda A. Richardson, A. Margaret Pevec.
      p. cm.
   Summary: "Real questions asked by children ages 10-14 underlie the topics in this guidebook. Each chapter discusses a theme's importance to the children, summarizes a recommended movie (including cautions), and provides both parent and child with talking points plus additional easy-to-do activities on matters of special concern to the family"--Provided by publisher.
   Includes bibliographic references and index.
   ISBN-13: 978-1-889242-31-6 (pbk.)
   ISBN-10: 1-889242-31-4 (pbk.)
   1. Children's questions and answers. 2. Communication in the family. 3. Children --United States--Attitudes. 4. Child rearing. 5. Motion pictures in child psychology. 6. Motion pictures and children. I. Pevec, A. Margaret. II. Title.
   HQ784.Q4R53 2007
   306.87--dc22

                                                                                    2007001287

Manufactured in the United States of America

10 9 8 7 6 5 4 3 2 1

For my daughters, Jenna and Logan

—R.A.R.

This book is dedicated to my five children: Jeffrey, Inara, Davina, Albert, and Monica. To paraphrase the inspired words of Kahlil Gibran, you are the precious arrows I have sent forth into the future. May each of you go swift and far, the perfect expression of that which only you can be.

—A.M.P.

Contents

Introduction 1

Definitions and Diversity 4

Tips for Using This Book 6

Movies for the Themes 7

Communicating with Your Preteen 10

PART I: Inside the Family

Chapter 1 This Clan is Our Clan:
The Extended Family 14

Chapter 2 Parents Are People, Too:
Each Parent as an Individual 24

Chapter 3 How It Began:
Parents as a Couple 36

Chapter 4 Me, Myself, and I:
Your Child's Beginnings 49

Chapter 5 Love Me Tender:
Support and Conflict Between
Parent and Child 61

Chapter 6 Roots and Wings:
Trust and Responsibility Between
Parent and Child 74

PART II: The Larger World

Chapter 7 Everybody Needs a Friend:
Peers and Friendships 89

Contents (continued)

Chapter 8   What's Love Got to Do with It?
Romantic Relationships **106**

Chapter 9   Making the Grade:
School **120**

Chapter 10   Nine to Five:
Work **132**

Chapter 11   Looking to the Future:
Adulthood **145**

Chapter 12   Is This Just the Way It Is?
Life **157**

Acknowledgments **168**

Appendix   450 Questions That Middle-School
Students Want to Ask Their Parents . . **170**

Selected Readings and Resources **186**

Activities Index **188**

Book Index. **189**

About the Authors **192**

Introduction

Young people between the ages of 10 and 14—no longer children but not yet young adults—are experiencing a multitude of changes. First, their bodies are changing dramatically. Between ages 12 and 14, adolescents average four inches of physical growth per year, and for the first time, sons and daughters can literally look their parents in the eye. They are too big to sit on a lap, and most wouldn't want to anyway. Cultural taboos against touching "mature" children mean that parents can no longer smother preteens with hugs and kisses.

Kids' thinking abilities are also undergoing a transformation. During the middle-school years, they begin to be able to see more than one side of an issue. They can question the reasons behind rules and point out contradictions between what parents say and what parents do. In addition, their social world is expanding. Now there are more friends, more teachers, more school and community activities to engage their interest and take up their time. That means other people, places, and experiences that they're having away from home take on a larger role in shaping their thoughts and decisions.

All of this means that when children reach the middle-school years, parent relationships with them are not the same as they used to be. Conflict increases, closeness decreases, and frustration can often result. All of these changes point to one important and undeniable fact: the middle-school years are a pivotal stage in the development of human beings.

The choices that middle-school students make and the experiences they have during these years will shape the course of their development through adolescence and into adulthood, and will greatly affect the kind of people they become. It is during this time of tremendous transition that young people need us, as caring parents, more than ever to support and guide them through the maze of changes and decisions they face. In matters of school, friendship, health, and happiness, the children who do the best are the ones who have good relationships with their parents.

It sounds so simple, doesn't it? To raise kids through the trying preteen years, parents just need to continue to love them, supervise them, and talk to them. But the reality is that in many families there is an alarming disconnect between parents and their young adolescent sons and daughters. Many parents don't know how or don't take time to talk with their middle-school children about important issues, and many kids feel unable to communicate with their parents. Data from large-scale national surveys by the Search Institute reveal that only one out of four youth report that their parents are approachable and available when they want to talk.

The results of this disconnect are evident in the numbers of kids involved in alcohol and drugs, violence, and other unhealthy behaviors. No wonder, then, that numerous professional organizations specializing in adolescent development (for example, the Carnegie Council on Adolescent Development, the Search Institute, the National Middle School Association) have identified re-engaging families with their children in early adolescence as a necessary priority.

But, as every parent of a middle schooler knows, this is easier said than done. When each question posed is answered with a one-word response, when parents find themselves talking to a closed bedroom door more often than to a child, when they hear "none of your business" or "leave me alone" or "go away" on a regular basis, it is easier to give up and let kids go their own way than to stand there and try to communicate.

Nonetheless, communication is the key, and many books are available to help parents learn to communicate more effectively with teenagers. There are also many books to help parents broach the topics they worry so much about because of their long-range consequences for children—things like HIV/AIDS, early pregnancy, or drug and alcohol abuse. All of these books are helpful and important, and some of our favorites are listed in the Selected Readings and Resources at the back of this book. However, what is lacking in many of the books written for parents is the voice of the young people themselves. What is it that 10- to 14-year-old children want their parents to talk about?

To find out, Dr. Rhonda Richardson, an educator with more than twenty years' experience in the field of adolescent development and herself the mother of two adolescent daughters, polled 1,124 middle-school students with the following inquiry: "If you could ask your mom or dad one question and know you would get an honest answer, what question would you ask?" The responding students, 520 boys and 604 girls between the ages of 10 and 14, were from urban, suburban, small-city, and rural areas. They represented low-, middle-, and high-income communities. The bulk of responses were from 11-, 12-, and 13-year-olds.

The surprising result of this research was that the questions kids want to ask their parents are mostly about relationships, and some of the most important relationship issues they want to talk about are within the family. The questions largely fell into twelve broad categories. For example, more than one hundred questions were about the parent-child relationship, including questions about the child's autonomy and budding independence, their parent's love for them, as well as questions about support, trust, and conflict. There were almost as many questions about the parent's childhood, life experience, and life perspective. There were nearly fifty questions about the extended family.

So, while you are asking your daughter things like, "How did you do on your math quiz?" or "Is your homework finished?" and getting one-word responses, she might secretly be wishing she could ask you questions like, "How happy were you when I was born?" "What were you like when you were little?" and "How much do you love me?"

We wanted to write a book based on this research to help parents initiate more meaningful conversations with their children during the middle-school years; to help parents nurture the bond and cement it more firmly in place prior to the years when hanging out with parents is the last thing a kid wants to do. We also thought it was important to provide a framework and activities to help initiate meaningful conversations. Since watching movies is a popular pastime, and we know from our own experience it is often a nonthreatening way for parents and teens to share time, we thought movies and conversation would be a winning combination. And voilà! *What Kids REALLY Want to Ask* was born.

In writing this book we have drawn on our own experiences and many years of reading and teaching about adolescence and parenting. While our insights and ideas represent a melding of many influences, from experiential to scholarly, we want to acknowledge several authors whose works have been particularly influential. They are Adele Faber, Grace Llewellyn, Elaine Mazlish, Alex Packer, and Laurence Steinberg. Their books are included in the Selected Readings and Resources section at the back of this book.

⭐ Definitions and Diversity

Families, like ice cream, come in many different flavors, all of them delicious. Some of you reading this book may be part of a traditional family, with a mom, a dad, and one or more children, who hope to find ways to spend quality time together. Some of you may be single moms or dads, who share custody and need to make the most of the time you spend with your child. Some of you may be single moms or dads handling the parenting job alone, who have just enough energy left at the end of a busy week to watch a movie. Some may be stepparents or unmarried partners of parents with preteens, who are looking for a way to be supportive. Some of you may be gay or lesbian parents, with or without a partner, who may or may not be biologically related to the child you are raising together. Some of you may be adoptive parents, who do not know much about the biological parents of your child. Some of you may be foster parents. Some of you may be aunts, uncles, youth group leaders, or school counselors who are looking for ways to interact more effectively with the children and their families that you care about. Welcome all! When we say "family," we mean *every* kind of family. When we say "parent," we are referring to any adult who cares about a child so much that they are reading this book.

Based on the research, this book is directed to families that include middle-school children. We use various terms for this group of younger people, including kids, middle-school children, middle schoolers, and middlers. We also use teens, preteens, young adolescents, and pre-adolescents. All of these are meant to refer to people moving through the transitional stage between elementary school and high school, roughly between 10 and 14 years old.

For simplicity's sake, we refer to one parent and one child when we discuss the topics in this book, and we alternate between the gender pronouns. There also may be younger brothers and/or sisters or more than one preteen in your household. We think this book can be used effectively with more than one child in a family, or even with a group of friends (see our note about monthly movie clubs near the end of the Tips section below). Some of the movies are suitable for younger children as well. We provide a cautionary summary of the language, sexual content, drug or alcohol activity, and violence in each movie so that you can decide if it is appropriate for all the children you want to include in your movie nights.

Some of the characters in the movies we've selected are older than middle schoolers, but we believe all the movies will be interesting and relevant to this age group as well as to adults. We've made a concerted effort, given the available resources, to make this book, the movies, and other activities inviting to a broad range of people and experiences. For example, we sought out movies that reflect some of the ethnic diversity of people living in the United States, although finding appropriate films with the variety we wanted was challenging. Middle class, working class, and poor families; urban, suburban, and rural settings are all represented. The protagonists are both boys and girls; in the case of platonic friendships, we suggest two movies to address differences related to gender. Films that portray populations such as family members with disabilities or families with gay or lesbian parents or offspring are still rare and are therefore not included. We hope more movies that reflect the incredible diversity of our country will become available in the near future so that a broader range of families can easily see themselves reflected in a book such as this.

★ Tips for Using This Book

What Kids REALLY Want to Ask is a guidebook, organized around watching movies together for the purpose of sparking meaningful conversations between you and the preteen in your life. The book contains twelve chapters. Each chapter explores one theme revealed through the research with middle-school students. Issues related to the family are addressed in the first six chapters, and broader relationship and life issues are covered in the last six. For each theme, we have identified one or two movies that reflect the kinds of questions kids seem to have about that topic. The chapters, themes, and movies are listed on the following page.

Each chapter begins with ten theme-related questions that were disclosed in the research. Then we provide brief information about the

PART 1: Inside the Family

Ch	Title	Theme	Movie
1	This Clan Is Our Clan	The extended family	Secondhand Lions
2	Parents Are People, Too	Each parent as an individual	Ferris Bueller's Day Off
3	How It Began	Parents as a couple	Back to the Future Mrs. Doubtfire
4	Me, Myself, and I	Your child's beginnings	Whale Rider
5	Love Me Tender	Support and conflict between parent and child	Smoke Signals
6	Roots and Wings	Trust and responsibility between parent and child	Bend It Like Beckham

PART 2: The Larger World

Ch	Title	Theme	Movie
7	Everybody Needs a Friend	Peers and friendships	Stand By Me (boys) Now and Then (girls)
8	What's Love Got to Do with It?	Romantic relationships	The Man in the Moon
9	Making the Grade	School	Akeelah and the Bee
10	Nine to Five	Work	October Sky
11	Looking to the Future	Adulthood	Real Women Have Curves
12	Is This Just the Way It Is?	Life	Pay It Forward

theme. Next is a short synopsis of the movie, including cautions about language, violence, drugs, alcohol, and sex, to help you decide whether it is suitable for your family. Based on the movie, we suggest questions for both you and your young person that will trigger ideas for a fruitful conversation.

There is also space for your child to write his own questions. These questions and their answers might help you understand where your child is confused or how he is feeling about something. The idea is to provide you and your child with topics and specific questions to ignite a dialogue, building a firm structure to help keep you close.

For those chapters where two movies are listed, you can decide which movie is more relevant to your child and family situation. For example, Chapter 3, "How It Began," offers a movie to help parents talk about how you and your child's other parent first met and decided to pair up. Even if you are no longer in a relationship with that other parent, we think it's important for kids to be able to talk about the early years of their parents' relationship. For those of you who are divorced, we offer a second movie choice in that same chapter to facilitate sensitive and honest discussion about marital conflict and dissolution.

Chapter 7, "Everybody Needs a Friend," also offers a choice because boys and girls have different interests when it comes to forming and keeping friendships. One of the movies is more appropriate to watch and discuss with a son, while the other is more suitable for a daughter.

In addition to one or two movies addressing the major themes, we have provided supplemental activities. These are simple ideas that don't take a lot of preparation or time, but your willingness to participate in them can help to elicit even more meaningful conversations.

Sometimes a child doesn't know what questions she has. For that reason, we've included an appendix listing 450 actual questions from the research. You might give the list to her and say, "Are there any questions on this list you would like to ask me?" Or you might randomly select a question and say, "Some kids your age had this question for their parent. Is this something you're curious about?" This could be fun during carpool time, on long road trips together, or at the family dinner table.

You can use this book in a variety of ways. For example, you can start at the beginning with Chapter 1, "This Clan Is Our Clan," by watching the movie together and initiating a conversation afterward based on our suggestions. Throughout the next month, you can bring up the topics or invite questions suggested within that chapter while eating meals or driving, or you can initiate some of the other activities we suggest. Maybe the first Saturday night of each month for a year becomes "movie night," in which you commit to exploring each subsequent chapter in turn.

If you prefer not to follow the chapters in numerical order, the twelve themes can also be addressed "as needed." That is, you can select a particular theme when something occurs that makes it relevant to your family experience of the moment. For example, if a death in the family has elicited more questions from your young person about his extended family, you might turn to Chapter 1, "This Clan Is Our Clan." Or if an incident at school has provoked a flood of tears or angst between your child and a friend, you might read Chapter 7, "Everybody Needs a Friend," and watch one of the movies together based on your child's gender. Chapter 8, "What's Love Got to Do with It?" would be helpful if you suspect the beginnings of a new romance are in the making and you want to open up that topic with your preteen.

Another approach, one which we highly recommend, is talking about the book with your preteen and inviting him to look through the list of themes and movies to select the one he is most interested in for each family movie night. This has the added advantage of cueing you in to what issues might be pressing for him at this moment.

Another creative way to use this book is to organize a monthly movie club with a group of other parents and preteens. After the movie, the kids can meet together in another room and brainstorm with each other the questions they most want to ask the adults. You can make a game out of it, rolling dice to decide who picks the first question out of a hat or who has to answer a question. Feel free to experiment. There is no "right way" to use this book.

The movies are available in both VHS and DVD formats at the large video stores and online rental services. They are also often available at libraries, used book sales, discount stores, or from friends with extensive video collections. Have fun! Be creative! Involve your young person!

★ Communicating with Your Preteen

Only 14 young people responded to Dr. Richardson's research question with statements like, "I know I can ask them anything right now" and "I can trust them not to tell and not to laugh." We hope *What Kids REALLY Want to Ask* will increase that tally by the number of young people *you* care about. Here are a few tips and reminders to help you create an open, inviting environment for your child to ask you questions.

★ Cultivate a support system for yourself. Parenting is the hardest job there is. To do it well and provide your children with the emotional support they need as they move through the preteen years, you need support, too. Especially helpful is a nonjudgmental partner or friend who will let you vent about your teen when you are angry or frustrated. It is helpful to have someone who can remember that both you and your child are good people struggling to grow and learn, despite whatever conflict might be happening. Search out parent support groups.

★ *What Kids REALLY Want to Ask* is a book designed to establish a level playing field on which parents and preteens can have meaningful conversations. The inherent power differential between parents and kids often gets in the way of honest and open communication. Work at eliminating criticism and judgments when using the suggestions in this book. Cultivate an atmosphere that says to your child, "There's no question you can't ask me. I will respect and take seriously any question you have." Your actions speak louder than words on this one. If you say you are open to any question but then indicate by your body language or your response that you don't mean it, it will be hard to regain your child's trust.

★ Take a cue from teenagers, who can be comfortable "hanging out" for hours together doing nothing in particular. If you've harmed your relationship with your child by losing your temper or by offering unsolicited or uncalled-for advice, "hanging out" on a regular basis might reestablish confidence in your teen so that he can feel safe talking with you again.

★ Try not to have any particular agenda. You may be ready to talk about the work world and stumble on a juicy discussion with your preteen about romance instead. Let the talk flow wherever it may. Take your cues from your child.

★ Let your child lead the conversation as much as possible. If she doesn't have anything to say, don't push it. Just make it clear you're open to talking about anything brought up by the movies, the activities, or the questions in the back of the book. Chances are she'll think it over and get back to you at a later time with anything that's on her mind.

★ When your preteen is talking, concentrate on listening, not on evaluating or judging what he says. Parents often feel they need to be imparting wisdom constantly. They also tend to make assumptions and jump to conclusions based on fears. Try to ask neutral, clarifying questions that encourage your child to talk, and work to keep your fears to yourself. Nothing stops a conversation with a kid more quickly than focusing on negative things he might get involved with in the future. The future is yet to be created. If you are listening with an open heart, it is more likely that his future decisions will take your values into account.

★ Practice asking open-ended questions—that is, ones that can't be answered with a simple yes or no. For example, saying, "What do you think about this idea of watching a movie together and talking about it afterwards?" works better than "Do you want to watch a movie?" if your goal is to elicit more than a one-word response.

★ Express how you're feeling using "I" messages. Better to say, "When you tell me you tried smoking, I feel scared because I know how addictive smoking can be and I care that you stay healthy" than to stop the conversation in its tracks by saying, "I forbid you to smoke. How could you do such a thing?!"

★ Be honest about your level of comfort with particular topics of discussion. If your child asks you something like, "When was the first time you had sex?" and you're not sure how you want to answer, it's better to say, "I'm not ready to talk about that. Could you give me some more time until I sort through my thoughts and feelings?" than to say "It's none of your business." Addressing sensitive topics for which you still have feelings of anger, grief, regret, or guilt can be tricky. It is fine to say you don't feel ready to discuss certain things because you still have too many emotions to talk about them rationally. Try not to be defensive. Remember, you are human and all humans have to deal with hard emotions at times. You might try saying something like, "That's something I just can't talk about easily. Could you write down your questions and give me some time to respond? It might take me a while, but I want to be honest with you."

★ Kids are listening even when they appear not to be. So, although giving your child positive reinforcement or assuring her of your love may sometimes feel like you're talking to the wind, do it anyway.

★ Touch is important to humans. Even though your preteen might often act as if he doesn't want hugs and kisses, it's a good bet that he still yearns for them. Find ways to touch. Offer your lap for his pillow while you watch a movie, stroke his back, or throw an arm over his shoulder. Request a hug before bed.

★ Let your middler know that your discipline is grounded in love. When your preteen challenges your rules concerning her safety or accuses you of being overprotective, it's a good idea to preface whatever you need to say with "You are one of the most precious people in my life, and I'm working really hard to make sure you stay safe and healthy." You can't tell your child too many times how much you love her.

★ Express humility. Nothing is more comforting to a child (or any of us) than to know that a parent has also made mistakes in life. It is more effective to convey the lessons you've learned from your mistakes than to deny that you've ever made them.

★ Trust your child to love you, warts and all.

We hope you and the young person you love will have many meaningful and heartfelt conversations based on the suggestions in *What Kids REALLY Want to Ask!*

This Clan Is Our Clan: The Extended Family

Chapter 1

Sample Questions Asked by Middle-School Kids

What is my family background?

Where did our family come from?

Do I have any relatives in other states?

Am I related to a famous person?

What were my great-grandparents like?

How did we get our last name?

Why don't you know your mom and dad, and why do you have a bad temper about it?

Why can't I ever see my uncle?

What would happen and where would I go if you died or we got taken away from you for some reason?

What does it feel like to lose a close relative?

⭐ A Few Things for Parents to Know

The potential for developing intergenerational relationships is growing as human beings live longer. It is becoming increasingly possible for adolescents to know not only their grandparents but also their great-grandparents. At the same time, families are more apt to be living far apart from each other as personal preference or opportunities call them away from the places they were raised. While some children live close to grandparents, aunts, uncles, and cousins and hear family lore from several sources, others live far away and have only parents to rely on for information.

As your child gains maturity, one of his tasks is to develop a personal identity, a sense of who he is. The extended family, therefore, is especially significant to him. During grade school his primary parent or parents were all he needed to understand his place in the family, but in middle school he will become more curious about how he fits into the larger family and how the family history has influenced who he is as an individual. A generational connection may help him feel grounded in the knowledge that he is part of a line of individuals with a unique history that includes his ethnic background, class background, and the influence of historic events and significant family incidents on his ancestors.

This chapter is more difficult to navigate if you have an adopted child for whom you can provide little information about blood relatives. It may also be difficult because often adopted children are cautious about asking questions since they don't want to upset their adoptive parents or appear ungrateful.

A conversation focused around the events in a movie gives you the opportunity to ask your child if she has questions about her biological family. If you have details about her birth parent(s) but haven't shared them, this might be a good time to broach the topic. If her origins have been thoroughly discussed, the message that she is wanted and loved and that you consider her an important member of your family cannot be expressed too many times. Your extended family still affects her life, and sharing your stories may help her feel more connected to them and ease her curiosity about her biological relatives. Children at this age want to feel like they belong. Giving her greater depth of information about your family history, and acknowledging that even though she is not biologically related, a bond of love and care exists for her, may soothe whatever issues she has and assure her of your willingness to talk about any concerns or questions she has whenever they occur. (Issues of adoption are also covered in Chapter 4.)

This chapter provides an opportunity to share thoughts about losing someone you love, to death or other circumstances. Were you close to a grandparent who died? Did you lose a parent when you were young? The cycle of life and death is natural to all living things and evokes deep emotion for people. Discussing the topic helps your child acquire useful information about how one might handle such an event, so give thought to what you want to communicate about death and grief with your child. (Chapters 8 and 12 provide additional openings for reflections and conversations about death.)

Several of the questions posed by the children in the research indicated sensitivity to family issues that are not openly discussed. Are there people you don't speak to in your family? If you decide to open a dialogue about this with your child, remember, it is best to explain things using "I" messages and to focus the conversation on your feelings rather than blaming the other person.

You can also decide how much information you're ready to provide and set a clear boundary. For example, you could say, "I felt hurt by some things that happened between your grandfather and me before you were born. They were pretty serious, and someday I'll share more with you. But right now, that's all I want to say." In this case, you could also let him know what you *are* willing to talk about, so there is no confusion. For example, you may be willing to talk about your early childhood but not your young adult years with a parent or sibling.

The purpose of this book is to have conversations with your child that will deepen your understanding and love for each other, providing a solid base of shared knowledge and feelings that will stand you in good stead when she is making stronger and stronger bids for independence in the years to come. Chances are if you trust her with the facts and the history of any discord that exists in the family, she will rise to the occasion of your sharing. It will also empower her to start forming her own understanding of the family dynamics.

It is not unusual for children as well as adults in families to feel different levels of affection towards other relatives. There may also be one or more family members with whom a child feels uncomfortable, awkward, or ill at ease due to personality, past behaviors, or lack of familiarity. This chapter and movie discussion will give you a chance to discover if your child would just as soon not have contact with a particular relative. If he doesn't bring that up in your conversation after the movie, you could broach the topic indirectly by talking about a relative you felt uncomfortable around as a child. Was there an uncle who drank too much at family weddings and always wanted to dance with you? An aunt who invariably pinched your cheek and asked the same silly question? A cousin who intimidated you? After telling your story, it's natural to say, "Is there anyone in our family you could do without?"

As young people move into early adolescence, their capacity for future-thinking and imagining various possibilities increases. Some will begin to wonder about who will take care of them if something happens to their parents. This is another poignant area of conversation that many parents hesitate to address. Yet part of that sense of belonging that children crave includes a reassurance of long-term care and connection.

It is especially important for single parents to address the issue and make appropriate arrangements for their children, particularly if there is no second parent in the picture and no one in the extended family lives close by. Talking about the plans you've made may relieve some anxiety. If you don't have a plan, you could ask about her preferences and together figure out who might be the best person to take over her care should the need ever arise.

Movie:	**Secondhand Lions**
Year:	2003
Length:	1 hour 50 minutes
MPAA rating:	PG
Key actors:	Michael Caine as Garth
	Robert Duvall as Hub
	Haley Joel Osment as Walter
	Kyra Sedgwick as Mae
Director:	Tim McCanlies

Movie Synopsis

Secondhand Lions is set in 1962 and tells the story of a 12-year-old boy named Walter. As viewers enter the story, his mother is driving him to the rural Texas home of her two uncles, Hub and Garth. The uncles don't recognize her and have never met her son. She convinces the uncles to take care of Walter while she is attending a school for court reporting and, after a brief visit, she leaves him there, alone with two old men he has just met. The uncles have no electricity, no telephone, and no TV. They are rich but live in a shabby old house. Their favorite sport is shooting at salesmen from their front porch. Despite their eccentricity, however, it is soon clear that they are tenderhearted men who respond to Walter's need for a home and attention. The three soon create a deep bond. Walter hears fantastic tales of high adventure and true love from his uncles. He also experiences the deep commitment and love his uncles have for each other and for him. When Walter's mom returns, he convinces her to let him stay with his uncles. The name of the film is derived from an old lion the uncles purchase to use for sport. The lion becomes a metaphor for the two elderly men whose sedentary lives suddenly take on new meaning as they nurture a young man to adulthood.

Cautions

Secondhand Lions contains minimal swearing *(damn, hell)*. Rifles are a prominent feature of the present-day events. For example, the uncles shoot at traveling salesmen but aim to miss, and no harm is done. They also use their rifles to fish! In another scene, the uncles and a family with three young children are all pointing rifles into a corn field where the old lion has hidden; they think she is mauling Walter. As Garth tells stories, Walter imagines his uncles in their younger days. In these scenes, Uncle Hub is a swashbuckling swordsman, fighting off attackers, rescuing his brother during a battle, and escaping with his true love on horseback. No one dies, and there is no blood. Early in the film, Uncle Hub questions his brother with, "Did you send for a hooker?" in reference to Walter's mother. In the final scenes of the film, viewers learn that the uncles have died in an airplane accident, but the actual crash and dead bodies are not shown.

Movie Talking Points for Parents

★ In *Secondhand Lions,* Walter had never met his great-uncles Garth and Hub. Do you have any relatives that your child doesn't know about? What can you tell him about these relatives? Who is the oldest person in your family? Where are your family's roots? What language did people in your family speak originally?

★ It is safe to say that Uncle Garth and Uncle Hub become Walter's favorite relatives. Do you have a favorite relative? What is it about this relative that makes him or her so special to you?

★ Uncle Garth and Uncle Hub had some exciting adventures in their younger years. Have you ever heard a story about something exciting, interesting, or even spooky that one of your relatives did or that happened to them?

★ Walter's great-uncles are eccentric. Who is your most eccentric relative and what makes him or her so interesting and unusual?

★ Uncle Garth and Uncle Hub had lots of money and lots of adventures. Do you have a relative who is wealthy or famous? What about any relatives who struggle with poverty, drug or alcohol addiction, mental illness, or physical disabilities? What do you want your child to know about them or the struggles they face?

★ Uncle Garth and Uncle Hub find it difficult to talk about their feelings of affection and old love affairs. What issues in your family do you find it hard to talk about?

★ Uncle Garth and Uncle Hub are brothers who obviously share a commitment to each other. Do you have a special brother or sister? What makes you feel close to that sibling? Have you always been close? If not, at what stage of your lives did the closeness develop and why? Can you think of a story you can tell your child about an adventure you and a sibling had together when you were teenagers or young adults?

★ Uncle Garth and Uncle Hub have some relatives who are only interested in their money and share no bonds of true affection. Do you have people in your family to whom you are not close? Are there relatives you try to avoid?

★ Uncle Garth and Uncle Hub die at the end of the movie, and Walter is sad. Has someone in your family died whom you miss very much? Were you with the person when they died? If not, how did you find out? Was there something you wish you could have said to him or her and didn't? If you went to the funeral, what happened there and how was that for you? What feelings did you have when this person died? How did you deal with your feelings? How long did it take to feel better?

For Kids: What Do You Think?

Secondhand Lions is about a 12-year-old boy who goes to live with two great-uncles. A great-uncle is the brother of a person's grandparent. How well do you know the people you are related to, like your grandparents, aunts, and uncles? Do you have a great-uncle or a great-aunt? Do you have questions about where your early relatives came from or where people in your family live now?

Here are a few questions to get an interesting conversation going with your parents about people you're related to. If you live with both your parents, *Secondhand Lions* is a good movie to watch all together so you can hear about both sides of your family, but watch out because it can get really complicated!

★ Uncle Hub and Uncle Garth soon become Walter's favorite relatives. Who is your favorite relative and why do you like him or her so much?

★ Uncle Hub and Uncle Garth seem to be in their late 60s or early 70s. Who is the oldest person you know in your family? What year was this person born? What do you know about his or her younger years?

★ Walter is quite a distance from home at his uncles' place. Have you ever had a chance to stay with a relative who lives far from you? Who would you like to stay with and what would you like to do during your stay? Where did your mom or dad spend time with relatives when they were young?

★ Uncle Garth and Uncle Hub were in the French Foreign Legion. Do you know whether any of your relatives were in the military or fought in a war? If not, ask your mom or dad what they know.

★ Walter's uncles turn out to be loving, kind, and caring, but not all relatives are like that. Are there any relatives that you wish you didn't have to see? What is it about them that makes you uncomfortable?

★ Walter decides he'd rather live with his uncles than go back to be with his mother. If something ever happened to your mom and dad, which relative would you like to live with and why?

✓ Your Turn

Now it's your turn to write down any questions you would like to ask one or both of your parents about people you're related to. What do you *really* want to know?

_____

_____

_____

_____

_____

_____

_____

💡 Activities

Parents and Kids: Collaborate on a list of interview questions for your oldest relative. If possible, plan to record the interview. In addition to all the factual questions (for example, the year they were born, where they grew up), be sure to ask some questions to find out more about this person's values and perspectives. Here are some examples:

* What invention that was created in your lifetime has had the greatest impact on your life?

* What famous person of your generation do you most admire and why?

* What historical event had the greatest impact on your personal life and why?

* What decision in your life has had the greatest impact on you?

Kids: Ask the oldest person in your family to show you any photographs he or she has. Are the photos labeled with names and dates? If not, offer to work with this relative to make sure all the photos are labeled for future generations.

Parents and Kids: Uncle Hub has some firm beliefs about things worth believing in: people are basically good; honor, courage, and virtue mean everything; power and money mean nothing; good always triumphs over evil; true love never dies. Spend some time discussing the values and beliefs that are most important to your family. Work together to design a coat of arms that reflects your family values.

Kids: Thanks to the Internet, more people are pursuing an interest in genealogy. Is there someone you know who has done genealogical research? If so, ask for a lesson in using his or her favorite genealogy website, and then see if you can find information about one of your ancestors.

Kids: Get a large sheet of paper and draw your family tree. Include everyone you know, alive or dead. Make photocopies of any photographs you have and add them to the tree as well. Talk to the oldest person in your family to help fill in any blank spots.

Parents Are People, Too: Each Parent as an Individual

Chapter 2

> ## Sample Questions Asked by Middle-School Kids
>
> What was your worst experience growing up?
>
> Were you ever pressured as a child, and by whom?
>
> What is your favorite thing to do?
>
> Did you have low self-esteem or high self-esteem when you were my age?
>
> When was the last time you enjoyed yourself?
>
> When you were my age, what bad things did you do with friends?
>
> How many illegal things have you done in your life? What were they?
>
> What's the stupidest thing you ever did?
>
> Have you ever experienced drugs? If so, what are they like?
>
> Have you ever gotten in trouble with the law?

A Few Things for Parents to Know

The middle-school years herald the time when young people begin to see their parents not just as caregivers but also as individuals with a past. Well represented in the research of kids' questions were those directly addressing the parents' lives during adolescence. Respondents with questions in this category seemed to want to hear about parents' experiences that might light their own path. You as a parent have already navigated the stages your child is now going through. While you might not remember it well or may want to forget it forever, you have a lot of information to share that might help your child on her own journey through the many decisions she will be making on her way to adulthood. While some of the questions asked by middlers seem to say, "Haven't you *ever* done anything wrong!?" many of them also imply a real desire to understand their parents as people: who you are, what you enjoy in life, what you most like to do, and who you were as a young person.

A good strategy for having a positive influence on your child throughout the teen years is to work at being an "askable" parent. If you haven't done so already, start now to create an atmosphere at home in which no topic is taboo, where no question is stupid, and where your own successes and failures as a person are part of the conversation. The implicit message in being so open is "I trust you to know me and to use my experiences to help guide your own life. I've been where you are now, and I trust that you will get through this time of many decisions with flying colors. You can ask me anything." Always resist the impulse to judge, criticize, or lecture. Children get messages about "right" and "wrong" behavior all the time from many sources. Your child knows alcohol, drugs, and tobacco are "bad." What he doesn't know is how to resist the social pressure to use those substances in middle school and high school. They are readily available; if he hasn't been already, he will soon be faced with deciding whether to use them. That's where your experience can be helpful.

Parents often wonder, "Won't talking about the 'bad' things I did give my child permission to do them?" Remember, you are in control of how you frame your earlier behavior and the resulting message you convey to your child. For example, it is possible to talk about your first party at which beer or alcohol was available and make it sound like either the best time of your life or the time when you first understood for yourself that one of the downsides of drinking is upchucking all over a friend or doing something so stupid while intoxicated that you became the laughing stock on Monday at school. Be sure to include in your discussion the awkwardness, the fear of not fitting in, or any peer pressure that was occurring. Was there someone you wanted to impress? Did you hope to be accepted into a particular crowd? Looking back, do you think you were driven by a high sense of self-confidence and esteem, or a low one? You can also let your middler know that whatever the choices you made when you were young, you can look back at those experiences now and feel differently about them. There may be some things you did as a teen that you now regret, or there may be things you wish you had done but didn't. What would you change if you could go back to middle school or high school now with all you have learned since then?

While reminiscing with your young person about your own teenage years, be sure to include talk about the fun and wholesome experiences you had. Kids often hear adults refer to adolescence as "the best years of my life," so your middler will want to know about your good times. What did you most enjoy doing? Who did you love to hang out with? How did you spend your free time in high school? Who were your favorite teachers or other adults with whom you had contact? What extracurricular activities were you involved in? Which of those interests have carried over into your adult life? What kinds of things do you like to do for fun now that you didn't know about then?

When you establish a relationship in which trust, honesty, and openness are the norm, your teen will be more likely to come to you to talk about matters with which she is struggling. The major task during adolescence is to develop a personal identity and to do so she needs to "try on" a number of behaviors to see what fits. Hearing about how you decided what was good for you and what wasn't provides her with useful information. She may be able to learn from your example how to size up the risks and benefits of choosing certain actions. Just saying,

"Don't do that," without backing it up with your life experience, will not convey as powerful a message and is likely to be ignored or dismissed.

While not all teenagers experiment with illicit drugs and alcohol, many do. It is likely that if adults did not commonly and openly use these substances and if they were not widely advertised and available, teenagers would not use them either. Every adult must take some responsibility for a culture in which substance use is the norm. According to a yearly survey called "Monitoring the Future" conducted by the University of Michigan, over 90 percent of 18-year-olds have tried alcohol and about 50 percent have used some kind of illicit drug. Because actions speak louder than words, how parents behave around these substances or speak of them to others conveys a powerful message. What values do you have about using drugs and alcohol? Do you take prescription medicine to help you relax or sleep, or do you look for natural substances for those purposes? Do you have a couple of glasses of wine when you get home from work, or a glass of fruit juice or tea? Do you offer friends a martini when they come to visit, or put on the coffee pot instead? Do you talk about how fun the party was where you got "smashed," or the stimulating conversation you had with someone new? As a parent of a preteen it's important to take stock of your own behavior. Is it congruent with your values and the messages you want to convey to your child? What sort of role model are you?

If you didn't do anything "bad" as a teenager, you still have stories to tell about how you made the decisions you made. What was the biggest influence on your behavior as a teenager? What values did you hold dear? Were you influenced more by your parents' values or by the values of other people or institutions outside the family? What topics were considered taboo in your family? Did that make you more keenly interested in them or less? Did your parents' style of parenting push you toward early experimentation with drugs and alcohol, or did it help you avoid these things? Teenagers are more likely to rebel against authoritarian parents who "lay down the law" and expect their word to be followed without question. On the other hand, democratic parents who provide a consistent and predictable balance between respecting their child as an individual while setting firm and clear boundaries are more successful. This book is all about adopting this style of parenting and developing a close, honest, open relationship in the preteen years that will carry you through your child's adolescence.

What if the decisions you made about alcohol, drugs, or tobacco as a teenager led to a life-changing experience like an early pregnancy, a serious car accident, a sexually transmitted disease, years of struggle with an addiction, or even incarceration? You may have spent a long time coming to grips with decisions you made as a young person. Who better to share that with your teen than you? It may be humbling to do so, but speaking honestly about such matters conveys a powerful message, especially if you can also articulate what you learned the hard way. Twelve-step programs are successful because people get to hear real personal experience, not just predictable homilies. You can trust your child to respect your honesty.

Now is a good time to reflect on the ways in which your child is both similar and different from you and try to uncover any subconscious expectations you may have about the choices he will make as he journeys through adolescence. Do you think he'll make healthy choices or unhealthy ones? How are the changes in our culture since he was born likely to influence his choices? You are not a young person now, so a good way to discover the challenges that your preteen faces that are different from those of your youth is by being curious about how it is for him in the world of chat rooms and instant messaging; in an age when incidents like Columbine have occurred with chilling regularity; when many middle-class teens have their own

TVs, computers, and cell phones; and where information about any topic is just a Google™ away.

Most teenagers feel close to their parents, respect their parents' judgment, and want to know their parents as individuals. While conflicts between parents and teens typically arise around mundane, day-to-day issues such as chores and homework, middlers will usually follow their parents' lead on matters of personal and family values. Sharing your younger self with your preteen—the fun and the adventures as well as the mistakes and the regrets—offers a powerful way for you to take that lead without alienating your young person.

On With The Show!

Movie:	**Ferris Bueller's Day Off**
Year:	1986
Length:	1 hour 42 minutes
MPAA rating:	PG-13
Key actors:	Matthew Broderick as Ferris Bueller
	Alan Ruck as Cameron Fry
	Jeffrey Jones as Ed Rooney
	Jennifer Grey as Jeanie Bueller
Director:	John Hughes

Movie Synopsis

Ferris Bueller's Day Off is a classic movie set in 1986 in and around Chicago. Ferris, a senior in high school, is having a hard time attending to his studies during his final year. He has already taken eight sick days off from school, but on the morning of another nearly cloudless day, he manufactures his ninth illness with all the cleverness, advance planning, and quick thinking of a truly motivated teenager. Ferris is beloved by the other students at school as much as he is despised by the principal, Mr. Rooney, whose only desire is to catch Ferris in the act of skipping school so that he can hold him back another year. Ferris's parents are oblivious to his shenanigans; his best friend, Cameron, cannot resist them; his girlfriend, Sloane, eagerly joins in them; and his sister is livid because he gets away with them. Meanwhile, Ferris blithely creates a joyful, never-to-be-matched day off from school with all the exuberance, self-confidence, and sense of inner freedom that both parents and preteens can appreciate and enjoy.

 Cautions

Words like *bullshit*, *ass*, *goddamn it*, and *fuck* (in various forms) are used throughout this movie by both the teenagers and adults; however, the profanity used by the principal and his secretary is directed towards the young people. For example, after the secretary has an interaction with Ferris's sister and the sister leaves the office, the secretary says, "What a little asshole." There are also several phrases involving street language for anatomy, like "you can smooch my big old white butt." Ferris is shown in the shower from the waist up and also delivers some dialogue in a men's room in which urinals are shown. The principal is portrayed as stupid, clumsy, vindictive, and so angry and out of control that he's ridiculous. Ferris's parents are depicted as completely gullible, naïve, and out of touch. No alcohol consumption or cigarette smoking is portrayed, although the school secretary is briefly shown sniffing a bottle of correction fluid, and a male teenager is sitting in the police station due to "drugs." There are one or two kisses between Ferris and his girlfriend, but no explicit sex is shown. There is one scene in which a drawing of a naked woman is displayed on a computer screen from some distance and another in which a sexy nurse, sent by Ferris's friends at school, shows up with an entourage at the Bueller's front door and recites a rhyme with sexual content.

Movie Talking Points for Parents

★ Ferris Bueller goes to elaborate lengths to convince his parents he is ill in order to skip school. Did you ever fake an illness so you wouldn't have to go to school? What illness did you simulate? Did your parents believe you? If you were successful, what did you do on your day off? Did you involve any of your friends?

★ Ferris and his friends do things they know their parents wouldn't approve of, such as skip school and borrow a car without asking. What are some things you did when you were a teenager that you knew your parents wouldn't approve of? What was the worst thing that happened because of that? Can you describe a time when you lied to your parents and got away with it?

★ Early in the movie Ferris says, in reference to licking his palms to simulate sweaty hands, "It's a little childish and stupid, but so is high school." Several scenes in the movie portray boring teachers and extremely bored students in the classroom. How did you feel about attending high school, especially in your senior year? Were you eager to get on with your independence, or were you content to play by the rules? Who was the most boring teacher in your high school? What made that teacher boring and what methods did you use to get through the class?

★ While Ferris has a strong and confident sense of self, Cameron is full of angst, anger, and trepidation about going along with Ferris and about life in general. Of these two characters, which one is more representative of you as a teenager? What can you tell your child about developing self-confidence and self-esteem? When you think about your own self-esteem, are you the same person you were as a teen or different? If different, what changed you? What parts of yourself as a teenager would you like to reclaim? What parts are still with you? What parts are you glad are gone forever?

* Ferris and his friends have some really fun adventures on their day off, from driving a really cool car to attending a baseball game to joining in a parade. What is your most memorable adventure—in or out of school—as a teenager? If given the choice, would you go back and relive your teenage years? Why or why not? As an adult, what are some things you like to do for fun?

* Ferris pressures his best friend, Cameron, to participate in his antics. What kinds of things did you feel pressured to do by other kids when you were a teenager? How did you respond to that pressure? Did you ever do the pressuring, encouraging friends to participate in mischievous behaviors?

* Mr. Mooney, the principal, is angry and out of control throughout the whole movie and is driven to "get Ferris" at any cost. Did any of the adults in your life ever act out of control or particularly mean? What was the atmosphere in your school and at home (strict, permissive, somewhere in between)? How was discipline handled?

* Although alcohol use is not shown or discussed in the movie and drug use is only briefly mentioned, teenagers are interested in their parents' early substance use. What can you tell your child about your use of alcohol, drugs, or tobacco as a teenager? What was the most common substance used among students at your high school? Did you feel pressured by peers to drink, smoke, or do drugs? At what age? How did you handle that?

* Ferris's sister is really angry with her brother until the very end of the movie when she helps him successfully escape any consequences for his behavior. If you have siblings, were you friends or enemies? Did you help each other, keep secrets and support each other, or ignore each other?

* Toward the end of the movie, Ferris's sister, Jeanie, is picked up by the police and taken to the police station for making a phony

phone call. Later, the police give chase when she is speeding while driving home. As a teenager, did you ever get picked up by the police for something you were doing? What happened that caused that? What did you learn from that experience?

 ## For Kids: What Do You Think?

Ferris Bueller's Day Off has been a favorite movie about teenagers since it came out in 1986. Ferris Bueller is portrayed as smarter and more clever than the adults around him, while the adults range from naïve to out of control. Ferris successfully accomplishes a day off from school by convincing his parents he's sick. Have you ever wondered how your parents were as teenagers?

Here are some questions based on the movie to give you some ideas for things to talk about with your parents.

★ Ferris lies to his parents and gets away with it, while his sister is treated much differently. If your parent has siblings, who do you think was the more adventurous based on how they are now? Do you think it would have been easy or hard to have siblings like your parent? What do you know about how well your parents got along with their siblings when they were your age? What do you think they argued about? Did they have any adventures together?

★ Ferris is so popular at his school that the whole student body seems to know he's sick, and some students go so far as to take up a collection for him. Do you think your parent was popular in high school? Based on what you know about your parent as an adult, which of the following crowds do you think he or she belonged to in high school: jocks, brains, nerds, populars, druggies?

★ What did you like most about Ferris Bueller? What did you like least about him? About Cameron? Do you think your mom or your dad as a teenager was more like Ferris, Cameron, or another character in the movie? What are your reasons for thinking this?

★ Cameron expresses a lot of anger towards his father, who seems to care more about his car than Cameron, but Ferris's parents are really attentive and concerned about Ferris. If you know your grandparents, do you think they were more like Ferris's parents or Cameron's dad?

★ Ferris's parents believe he is truly sick, even though he has missed eight previous days of school. How do you think your mom's or your dad's parents might have handled that?

★ Having fun is Ferris's only concern on his perfect day off, and he seems to have plenty of money. Knowing what you know about your mom or dad now, how do you think she or he would have spent a day playing hooky from high school if money were no object?

★ The movie ends before we find out what happens when Cameron's father gets home. What do you think would be an appropriate punishment for Cameron? What do you think happened to your mom and dad when their parents caught them doing something they weren't allowed to do? What category of "bad" behavior do you think your dad or your mom was most drawn to in high school, for example, ditching school, smoking, doing drugs, drinking alcohol, playing pranks, "borrowing" someone's car? Do you think teens today do similar things?

✓ Your Turn

Now it's your turn to write down any questions you would like to ask one or both of your parents about their teenage years. What do you *really* want to know?

_____

_____

_____

_____

_____

_____

_____

_____

💡 Activities

Kids: Ask your aunts, uncles, and/or grandparents what they remember about one of your parent's teen years, especially about getting in trouble at school or at home, and then ask your parent what he or she remembers about the same incidents.

Parents and Kids: Have a discussion about your perfect Ferris Bueller day—what would you do, where would you go, who would you bring along? Be sure to discuss whether "being bad" (like playing hooky from school or work) would make it more fun. Then, plan to do it together!

Parents and Kids: Take a walk down memory lane with your young person by looking at photographs, videos, or yearbooks from your teen years and telling your young person which crowd each of the people you knew belonged to and anything you remember about them. If fellow students wrote in your yearbook, read through all the comments together. If you kept a personal journal or diary and you still have it, get it out and read through it together.

Parents and Kids: Type "best school excuses" into an Internet search engine and spend a few minutes looking at the results and laughing together! Then, for balance, look up "best work excuses."

Kids: Write a *Ferris Bueller's Day Off* manifesto explaining why every teenager should be able to take one day off each school year for no reason whatsoever except to have fun.

How It Began: Parents as a Couple

Chapter 3

Sample Questions Asked by Middle-School Kids

How did you meet?

What made you fall in love with each other?

How long have you been together?

When and why did you decide to get married?

Are you glad you married each other?

Why do you guys fight sometimes?

Did you have anybody else that you loved?

Could we move closer to my dad so I could see him more often?

Why did you get divorced (or separated)?

Have you ever thought about getting remarried?

A Few Things for Parents to Know

Whether you live in an intact family, a divorced family, or one in which both parents are not present for other reasons, children are curious about their parents' early relationship. Discussing this topic with your middler can be complicated, so we have included two movies to help you address the issues in your family. We recommend that you watch *Back to the Future* to discuss your early relationship with your child's other parent. We have also included *Mrs. Doubtfire* to address the issue of divorce. Use your personal situation to decide whether to watch both movies or just one.

Discussion of your relationship with your child's other parent is important for several reasons. It provides the opportunity to fill your child in on the family history that explains her own existence. It also opens the door to conversations about choosing an appropriate mate. As you share details about your own early relationship, you can point out qualities and behaviors that you have learned can lead to success or failure in building a fulfilling long-term union. Discussing this topic can also help your child to notice the ways in which she is similar to or different from each of her parents in terms of whom she is attracted to, or the qualities in another person she might look for as she defines her own identity. And it can help your young person develop a realistic understanding of the importance of compatibility, compromise, and communication for maintaining a loving relationship.

Divorce is of particular interest to children in this day and age, both in intact families and divorced ones. It is best to discuss it openly. If your family is intact, any arguments your child overhears between the adults in the household might cause him concern. If divorce is the furthest thing from your mind, this could be a good opportunity to reassure your preteen that despite any difficulties, you are both committed to your relationship and to him. It would help if that message came from each of you individually, as well as being explicitly stated when you are all together. To assist you in discussing the topic of divorce, one of the two movies offered in this chapter deals specifically with that issue. We think this alternate movie will be of particular interest to parents who are no longer in a relationship with their child's other parent.

If you are separated or divorced from your child's other parent, your early relationship is still relevant to her life. Opening up the topic of your early relationship with your former partner can become a stepping stone to more honesty in general about what went awry, the choices you made, and how you might have done things differently. It can also lead to great conversations about how personality or value differences can present challenges to a relationship. Being openly self-reflective about your own learning process in relationships can go a long way toward helping your child make more informed choices. It is not appropriate to criticize her other parent. Try to focus on expressing your personal feelings using "I" messages. For example, "I thought I was in love with your father, but I really didn't give our relationship enough time to understand what that meant before we got married."

If it is too soon to talk about your divorce openly, be explicit about the boundaries of what you are willing to discuss with your preteen at this time, but also leave the door open for future conversations with him when your feelings are more in control. It's important to emphasize that your adolescent was not the cause of any of your difficulties. It is also fine to say you don't feel ready to address certain topics because you still have too many emotions to talk rationally. Try not to be defensive, but, again, use "I" messages and feelings. For example, "I still feel hurt and confused about the divorce, and it's hard for me to talk about it with you." You might offer to respond to written questions, explaining that you need time to think through your answers. He will appreciate your willingness to communicate and also your human vulnerability. Whatever the situation is in your household, try to convey an atmosphere of openness and honesty.

Prior to movie night, you might want to give some thought to what you want to share with your preteen about your early sexual exploration. Are you willing to talk about the decisions you made about having sex and how they have affected your life? Would you like her to emulate your sexual behavior or avoid it? What things do you wish you had considered more carefully? Are there things you wish someone had told you about relationships or sex that would have made it easier for you? (Sex is also discussed in Chapter 8.)

Movie: **Back to the Future**
Year: 1985
Length: 1 hour 51 minutes
MPAA rating: PG
Key actors: Michael J. Fox as Marty McFly
               Christopher Lloyd as Doc Brown
Director: Robert Zemeckis

Movie Synopsis

The classic movie *Back to the Future* introduces us to 17-year-old Marty McFly, a skateboarding high schooler who is good friends with Doc Brown, a crazy inventor. They live in a small town. Doc Brown converts a DeLorean car into a time machine and sends Marty into the past to the time when his parents were attending high school. Marty accidentally meets his future mother, and she starts having romantic notions about him. Marty realizes that if his mother doesn't connect with his father, he will not be born! Marty figures out a way to help his future parents have their first date. Then he and a much-younger Doc Brown successfully power up the DeLorean so Marty can travel back to his present. There he gets a big surprise when he learns how his involvement in his parents' first date had startling results for his family.

Cautions

The movie has some brief violence when Libyan terrorists racing through town attack Doc Brown in a parking lot where he is readying his time machine for its maiden voyage. They drive crazily around the parking lot, shooting guns out of the sunroof of their van. Doc Brown is shot in the chest and falls to the ground, but no blood is shown.

In addition to this violence, which figures prominently in the plot, there is occasional swearing *(holy shit, you son of a bitch, goddamn it)* by various characters throughout the movie. There is no explicit sex or nudity, although one scene involves a bully manhandling a girl in a car. There is a brief scene that portrays minimal alcohol use, smoking, and reference to reefer. In one scene a teenage boy calls an African-American man a spook.

 ## Movie Talking Points for Parents

★ Marty's dad is pretty nervous and has a great deal of trouble asking Marty's mom for a date. Marty's mom seems much more comfortable. Was it easy or difficult for you to ask someone for a date when you were younger? Would you say you were a late bloomer, an early bloomer, or average?

★ Marty's mom and dad meet while they're in high school. How did you meet your preteen's other parent? Was it a chance encounter that brought you together? Did friends introduce you? How old were you? Where did you have your first kiss? Did you date for a while before you became more seriously involved? What things did you most enjoy doing together at the beginning of your relationship?

★ Marty's parents hang out at the local burger joint. Where did you like to go when you were first dating? Who were your closest friends? Did your friends support your relationship or discourage it? Why?

★ Marty is growing up in the same town as his parents. If you live in the same town now, what has changed since you met your partner? If you live in a different town, have you ever gone back to where you met? How does it feel to you now?

★ Marty's mom isn't interested in his dad until his dad defends her against the bully who is harassing her. Did you ever have any doubts about whether or not you should become a committed couple? Were either of you involved with someone else when you met? Were any hearts broken when you became a couple?

★ Marty is worried that if he doesn't intervene, his parents will not get married and have him. Was there ever a point in your relationship where things might have resulted in a vastly different outcome? Is there anything you would change about your early time together as a couple?

★ Marty's parents don't talk much together in their high school encounters. Did you find it easy or difficult to talk to your partner in the early days? Was it hard or easy to express feelings with each other? Has this improved or not over time? What have you learned about communicating more effectively with each other since then?

For Kids: What Do You Think?

Back to the Future tells a fun story about Marty McFly and how he travels into the past and meets his parents in high school just when they are beginning their relationship. How much do you know about your parents' early relationship? Now is the time to ask any questions you have.

To get your creative juices flowing, share your answers to the following questions with your parent or parents and see what they say!

★ Marty's mom only seemed to notice his dad after his dad defended her against the bully. What do you think your parents liked about each other when they first met?

★ Marty's dad was a pretty weird guy. What do you think your parents found weird about each other when they first met?

★ Marty gets to travel back to the time when his parents were in high school. If you could travel to the time when your parents were younger, when would it be? What would you like to witness in their early relationship together?

- ★ Marty's parents were in high school when they met. If you could change something about the how, when, or why your parents got together, what would it be?

- ★ At the beginning of the movie, Marty's parents don't seem very happy, but at the end they have changed dramatically for the better. If you could change something about how your parents are with each other now, what would it be and why?

- ★ When *Back to the Future* was made, fewer people got divorced, but now it is common. If your parents are divorced, what do you think caused them to split up? Would you like them to get back together? Why or why not? How does their divorce affect your life?

- ★ Marty didn't realize how much his involvement in his parents' early relationship would change his family. If you could wave a magic wand and have all your dreams come true, what would you change for your parents?

✓ Your Turn

Now it's your turn to write down any questions you would like to ask one or both of your parents about their early relationship. What do you *really* want to know?

_____

_____

_____

_____

_____

_____

_____

On With The Show!
(Film 2 of 2)

Movie:	Mrs. Doubtfire
Year:	1993
Length:	2 hours 5 minutes
MPAA rating:	PG-13
Key actors:	Robin Williams as Daniel Hillard and Mrs. Doubtfire
	Sally Field as Miranda Hillard
Director:	Chris Columbus

Movie Synopsis

The classic, heartfelt comedy *Mrs. Doubtfire* tells the story of the Hillard family as they adjust to the parents' divorce. Miranda Hillard, a successful corporate architect and mother of three children (ages 5, 12, and 14), announces in the midst of an argument with her husband, Daniel, that after 14 years of marriage she wants a divorce. Daniel is a comedic voiceover actor and fun-loving dad who is crazy about his children and devastated at the prospect of breaking up the family. After the judge awards custody of the three children to Miranda and only one weekly visitation day to Daniel, the devoted father uses his creativity and talents to devise a plan that will enable him to have daily contact with his children. In response to Miranda's classified ad seeking a nanny, Daniel disguises himself and adopts the persona of a wise and warm-hearted British widow, and is hired for the position under the name Mrs. Doubtfire. What follows is a series of humorous and touching scenes as Daniel dispenses fun, life wisdom, and love to his children while at the same time helping both himself and Miranda gain greater understanding and appreciation for the depth of love between parent and child that transcends the pain of a marital break-up.

Cautions

At the beginning of the movie there are several minutes of arguing between Daniel and Miranda with a few swear words *(piss off, goddamn)* but no physical violence occurs. There is no sex or nudity in the film, although there are a few sexual references when Mrs. Doubtfire is conversing with Miranda about her new boyfriend, Stu (the words *foreplay* and *celibacy* are used but no elaboration is given). Later when Mrs. Doubtfire is speaking with Stu about Miranda, there are several sexual innuendos unlikely to be understood by most 10- to 14-year-old viewers. There is one restaurant scene that portrays Mrs. Doubtfire drinking alcohol to the point of intoxication and creating a socially embarrassing situation for Miranda and the children.

Movie Talking Points for Parents

★ Miranda and Daniel divorced after 14 years of marriage. Were you ever married to your child's other parent? If so, how long were you married?

★ The children in *Mrs. Doubtfire* learn of their parents' decision to divorce by overhearing an argument between Miranda and Daniel. How did your child first learn of your decision to divorce? If you could go back to that moment in time, what would you do differently and/or what would you do the same?

★ In many cases of divorce, the topics that spouses fight about are not the core source of unhappiness in the marriage. In the movie, Miranda and Daniel argue about Daniel's irresponsible behavior and messy house on the day he throws a twelfth birthday party for their son Chris, but the underlying problem is a basic incompatibility between them. What would you like your child to know about the real reason(s) you and his other parent got divorced?

★ In the movie, sole custody of the children is awarded to Miranda on the grounds that Daniel has no employment. He is granted visitation with the children every Saturday. What custody and visitation arrangements were made by the court in your situation? How were these decisions made?

★ Daniel is unhappy with the limited amount of visitation the court awards him and desperately wants to spend more time with his children. How much time does your child spend with her other parent? Do either you or the other parent actively try to arrange for more time to spend with her?

★ In the movie, 12-year-old Chris blames himself for his parents' divorce, saying, "I never should have had a birthday; this never would have happened." Do you think your child ever feels like the divorce was his fault? What can you say to him to reassure him that it wasn't?

★ Miranda says she didn't like who she was when she was with Daniel. In what ways does your child's other parent bring out the worst in you? What are three positive things you can tell your child about her other parent?

★ In the movie, Miranda and Daniel get along better when they are apart than they did when they were living together. Are there any ways in which you get along better with your child's other parent now than you did when you were together?

For Kids: What Do You Think?

Mrs. Doubtfire tells the story of a divorced dad going to extreme and funny measures to be able to spend time with his children. The subject of divorce is hard for many parents to talk about, and children often have a lot of unanswered questions about why their parents got divorced. Many children feel angry and sad when parents are divorced, but they don't know how to share these feelings with their parents. There may be a lot of things you wish you knew about your own parents' divorce. You may have a lot you wish you could to say to them about how it makes you feel. Now is the time to ask any questions and express any feelings you have.

To get you started, share your answers to the following questions with your parent or parents and see what they say!

★ In the movie, the 12-year-old son, Chris, blames himself for his parents' divorce, saying, "I never should have had a birthday; this never would have happened." What thoughts like that have you had about your parents' divorce?

★ What do you think is the reason the parents in the movie got divorced? What do you think is the reason your own parents got divorced?

★ The three children in the movie feel sad and miss their father after he moves out of the house. Can you describe a time when you have missed your other parent? What do you miss about the parent you don't see as often? When is the last time you felt sad because your parents are divorced?

★ The children in the movie want their parents to get back together. They say to their dad, "Can't you just tell Mom you're sorry?" If you could, would you want to get your parents back together? What would be good about that? What would be bad about that?

★ When Mrs. Hillard is talking to Mrs. Doubtfire about her ex-husband, she begins to say hurtful things about him in front of the children. Has one of your parents ever said critical things to you about your other parent? If so, what feelings did you have afterwards?

★ At the end of the movie, Mrs. Doubtfire replies to a letter from a child whose parents are divorced and offers words of support and advice. If you could talk to other kids whose parents are getting divorced, what advice would you give to help them feel better about the divorce?

★ At the end of the movie, Miranda is ready to set aside her differences with Daniel and do what is best for the children by letting him take care of them every day after school. What differences or disagreements do you wish your parents could set aside?

★ While posing as Mrs. Doubtfire, Daniel finds lots of fun activities to do with his children. What are some activities you would like to do with the parent you don't see as often?

✔ Your Turn

Now it's your turn to write down any questions you would like to ask one or both of your parents about why they are not together any more. What do you *really* want to know?

_____

_____

_____

_____

_____

_____

_____

_____

💡 Activities

Parents and Kids: Play "Two Truths and a Lie" around the dinner table. Each adult takes a turn telling two truths and a lie about their early relationship. The young people have to guess which statement is the lie. The person who guesses correctly gets an extra helping of dessert or is excused from after-dinner chores!

Kids: On a large sheet of paper draw a timeline of your parents' relationship and interview them for the dates. Be sure to include the date of their first meeting, their first kiss, their decision to become a couple or get married, your birth date and your brothers' or sisters' birth dates, moves from one house or place to another, changes in jobs, or any other important events from your family's history.

Kids: Interview several people to gather more details about your parents' early relationship. For example, ask your grandparents or aunts and uncles what they remember about how your parents met.

Parents: Show your child pictures of you and your child's other parent around the time you met. Write a short description of each picture including when and where it was taken.

Kids: Team up with your siblings to organize a "This Is Your Life" party for your parent or parents, acting out memorable scenes from their early life together. Make it as funny as possible!

Parents: Make a list called "Things I Know Now That I Wish I Knew Then About Choosing a Partner." The rule is that the list can have only "I" messages about what you have learned, and it cannot mention the other parent or say anything critical of anyone, including yourself. The list can be expanded as thoughts about the topic arise.

Me, Myself, and I:
Your Child's Beginnings

Chapter 4

Sample Questions Asked by Middle-School Kids

Why am I not anything like my mom?

Am I adopted?

What really happened when I was born?

What was I like when I was a baby?

Why did you pick my name?

Was there anything wrong with me when I was born?

How happy were you when I was born?

Did you want me to be a boy or a girl?

Did you want to have me?

Why did you have me?

⭐ A Few Things for Parents to Know

What is the earliest memory you have of yourself? Do you recall anything from when you were an infant or toddler? Have you heard stories or seen photographs of yourself as a young child? Most of us want to have a sense of our personal history; we want to know our own life story, including where we came from and how we got to where we are. It is often during early adolescence that this curiosity about our early life first emerges. The rapid and remarkable physical changes during puberty may prompt a middler to begin wondering how she looked as a baby and notice ways she is similar to or different from her parents, siblings, and other relatives. Changes in thinking also contribute to a new awareness of self, and preteens may spend a lot of time thinking about the question "Who am I?" Imagining how things might now be different if her childhood had been different is also possible during these years. She is likely to conjure many questions about her early life in order to fill in any missing pieces and gain insight into how she has come to be the person she is today.

Kids in our research wanted to know their birth stories: why their parents made the decision to have a child, how their names were chosen, whether their births were complicated. This is the time to share with your child the story of his own birth and his arrival in your family. Was this a joyous time for you? Was it the culmination of many months or years of planning and anticipating? Was it something unplanned but still wanted? Were there medical, family, or financial difficulties that made this a challenging time for you? Whatever your personal story, it is important to convey to your middler by your words, body language, and tone of voice that you can't imagine what life would have been like without him since he was born. He needs to know that even if there were struggles around that time, it had nothing to do with him or how much you love him.

One question that emerges for some young adolescents is whether or not they are adopted. In the research, a total of nine boys and girls asked about this. When your biological child poses this question, it may not mean she truly believes she is adopted, but adoption may offer a plausible explanation for any differences between you that are especially problematic. Bringing this out into the open could be helpful in discovering the ways she feels alienated and how you can begin to address the situation.

Of course, if your child *is* adopted, knowing about and integrating his biological background is essential to his sense of well-being. If you are the parent of one of the 1.6 million adopted children in the U.S., helping him feel comfortable embracing his "dual" parentage is one of the most important and challenging things you will be called upon to do. As an adoptive parent, it's important to remember that his talking about his adoption and asking about his birth family does not mean he is rejecting you. It is a normal, developmental step specific to adopted children, who have a bigger job answering the question "Who am I?" than those who live with their biological families. An adopted child is forced to deal with the reality that two families exist and have influenced his life. This will never change, and somehow he must incorporate the knowledge of both families into his understanding of self. It is a reality that he will live with forever. Your openness and willingness to help in any way will assist him in profound ways that are bound to draw you closer.

Hopefully, you have carefully laid the groundwork in your child's earlier years by speaking openly and frequently about her adoption so that she has integrated that reality into her concept of self and knows that talking about this with you at any time is perfectly okay. If you haven't done this, now is an excellent time to start. Reading this chapter and watching this movie together may help.

By middle-school age, your adopted child is ready to start assimilating some of the complexity of his specific situation into his understanding of who he is. One helpful message to convey at this point is that he may have feelings about his birth parents' relinquishment of him that are separate from feelings or issues about being a member of his adoptive family. Making that distinction can help him to manage, think about, and express his feelings better. It also provides you the opportunity to honestly tell your side of the story—what led you to the decision to adopt, what steps you took to find him, how long you had to wait for him, how you felt while you were waiting, how you shared the process with your parents or other family members and friends, the delight with which you received him into your family. It also allows you to ask open-ended questions specific to each side of the adoption equation to discover what issues might be troubling him at any particular time. While you may have read him books when he was very young that told a specific adoption story, now is the time to refrain from *telling* and to concentrate on *listening*. What is really on his mind? What can you help him with? If it is possible to be in touch with his birth mother, consider arranging a meeting. If a meeting isn't possible, but there is a way to send the birth mom a letter, you might suggest he write to express what he's thinking about, what he wants to ask her, and how he feels. Even if this letter can't be delivered, you can encourage him to write it anyway and save it for the time when finding his birth mother might become possible. Helping him make this letter writing a ritual on Mother's Day can assist you both in paying attention to the special needs he has. It also provides him with a record of how his thoughts about his relinquishment changed over time, which will be valuable to him when he's older.

Early adolescence is the time when adopted children start fantasizing about birth parents. Your child may imagine her birth parents to be the "perfect mom" and the "perfect dad," especially when things between you are rocky. Again, bringing this into a conversation by asking a question like, "What thoughts do you have about your birth mom or dad?" and then offering any facts you know about them might help with the assimilation process. It is also common for adopted children to feel they don't belong in their adoptive family or to develop a persona that "fits" even though it isn't authentic. One idea to ease this is to engage in activities with her that she finds interesting, especially if they are different from what you might choose. For example, you may encourage her to select an activity once a month in which the rest of the family participates or ask for her input to make holidays special for her. This is good advice to encourage and support the uniqueness of biological children as well.

Perhaps you are one of the approximately 800,000 grandparents who are raising a grandchild without the presence or assistance of the parents. Similar to adopting a child from a family you don't know, talking openly and in a positive manner about the circumstances that led to this reality will let your grandchild know it is okay to ask questions about his beginnings and can help him find some missing pieces in his search for his identity. If the circumstances around your grandchild being placed with you are unfortunate, then you will want to tell him what you can while still allowing him to honor and respect his birth parents. There may be some truths that would be too difficult for him to hear—truths about early mistreatment or even abandonment by his parent. It's not necessary to tell him things that would cause him to see his birth parents in a negative light. Rather than dwelling on the reasons he was taken away from or given up by his birth parents, focus on the message that you are committed to him and that you're happy he's with you now.

This chapter also provides an opportunity to acknowledge the significance of gender as an influence in your child's early upbringing. She will be interested in knowing how your preparations for her and her early years were shaped by gender expectations. For instance, did you choose items that were pink to represent a girl, or did you select gender-neutral colors for her like yellow and green? Did you choose a distinctly "girl" name or opt for a name that would be appropriate for either gender? Did you hear messages from relatives about hoping for a "grandson" or a "niece"? From a very early age parents and other caregivers have different expectations about what it means to be a boy or a girl and may treat their children accordingly. For example, rough and tumble play may be tolerated or even encouraged in sons but not daughters; crying may be approved of for girls but not boys. What do you think and how do you feel about these issues related to gender, and what can you share about them with your child?

Kids in early adolescence tend to be very much aware of gender and the associated expectations. The physical changes of puberty accentuate the basic biological differences between boys and girls. Some young adolescents may want to dress in ways that emphasize these differences, for example, girls choosing clothing and wearing makeup and jewelry to look "pretty" and boys opting for a more athletic look. Gender role expectations also are reflected in middlers' behavior. There may be differential treatment of boys and girls in the home. Chores may be assigned based on gender, with boys doing outside jobs such as washing cars or mowing the lawn and girls helping inside with laundry and dishes. Children may wonder whether parents would have preferred another gender. They may be concerned about or frustrated by the fact that certain opportunities are more or less available to them depending on their gender.

There is a wealth of important information to share with your child having to do with her arrival in your family. Nothing is more interesting than our own stories about how we came to be.

On With The Show!

Movie:	**Whale Rider**
Year	2002
Length:	1 hour 41 minutes
MPAA rating:	PG-13
Key actors:	Keisha Castle-Hughes as Paikea
	Rawiri Paratene as Koro
	Vicky Haughton as Nanny Flowers
	Cliff Curtis as Porourangi
Director:	Niki Caro

Movie Synopsis

Filmed in New Zealand, *Whale Rider* tells the story of a young Maori girl named Paikea, who is being raised by her paternal grandparents after her mother and twin brother died during childbirth. Paikea believes she is destined to become the next leader of her people. According to legend, the first leader of the Ngati Konohi tribe arrived on the back of a whale over a thousand years ago, and since that time every subsequent leader has been a firstborn male. Paikea's grandfather Koro, who is to choose the next leader, is bound by tradition and patriarchy, and he resists his granddaughter's wishes to be trained in the warrior ways and customs of her people. With determination and strength, Paikea fights to prove her worthiness to her grandfather and to claim her destiny as the next whale rider.

Cautions

Although rated PG-13, there is very little for parents to be concerned about in this movie. The opening scene depicts a woman giving birth and subsequently dying, but there is no blood involved. Alcohol use is alluded to briefly when Paikea visits her uncle at his home. When Koro is teaching a group of young boys about the warrior ways, he tells them that if they break the ancient chant then "your dick will drop off; so hold on to your dicks." This is presented as a humorous moment in the film as the young boys snicker and grin in response to his warning. There is no sex, violence, drug or tobacco use in the film.

Movie Talking Points for Parents

★ *Whale Rider* opens with a scene of a mother giving birth. What can you tell your child about the circumstances of his birth? For example, what time of the day or night did labor begin? What were you doing at the time? If you went to a hospital, what made you decide it was time? If you had your child at home, did a midwife attend the birth? If so, at what point did she arrive? Who attended the birth? Who were the first people you called when he was born?

★ Paikea's mother and newborn twin brother both die in childbirth. Were there any medical complications surrounding your middler's birth? What can you tell your child about this? Was your child born with any special conditions or concerns?

★ When Paikea is born, everyone in the family is waiting for a firstborn boy. Her grandfather Koro in particular is disappointed that she is a girl. Prior to your middler's birth, how important was it to you that you have a boy or a girl in particular? If you had a preference, which were you hoping for—a boy or a girl? What are some family traditions or patterns that contributed to this preference for you (for example, would this be the first grandson or granddaughter)?

★ Paikea's mother dies in childbirth, and her father is too emotionally distraught to take care of her, so she is being raised by her grandparents. If your middler is adopted, what can you tell him about the circumstances through which he came to be your child?

★ Shortly after Paikea is born, her uncle and grandparents arrive at the hospital to see her. Who was present when your young person was born or arrived in your family? What family members and friends made visits to welcome her after her arrival? What gifts did you receive for her?

★ Paikea's father is very happy about her birth but also is devastated at the loss of his wife and his newborn infant son. What emotions did you feel at the time of your young person's birth or his arrival in your home? What made you especially happy at that time? How did you celebrate his arrival? What, if anything, made you sad or worried?

★ Paikea's father names her after the legendary ancient tribal leader. Is there any special significance to the name you chose for your middler? How did you choose that name? What other names might you have chosen? If someone else was involved in choosing a name, were you in complete agreement or not? Does the name have any family significance?

★ As a young girl, Paikea loves spending time with her grandfather Koro, riding on his bicycle handle bars, talking to him about the legends of their people. She is a determined young girl, and her grandmother's friends refer to her as "bossy." What was your middler like when she was a child? What were some of her favorite activities? Who did she enjoy playing with and spending time with? What was her personality like? Can you recall any particularly funny moments during her early years? Was there a talent or a characteristic that you noticed early in her life that has developed over time? Did you ever have a sense of destiny for this child?

For Kids: What Do You Think?

Whale Rider tells about a 12-year-old girl named Paikea, who is being raised by her grandparents because her mother died in childbirth and her father was too emotionally distraught to care for her. How much do you know about your own birth story? Do you sometimes wonder what you were like when you were a baby? Now is the time to ask any questions you have about your beginnings.

To get your creative juices flowing, share your answers to the following questions with your parent or parents and see what they say!

★ Paikea lives in a community in which there are very clear ideas and traditions about what behaviors are acceptable for boys and for girls. For example, she is not allowed to be trained in the warrior ways because she is a girl. What are some messages you have gotten about things you can or cannot do because of being a boy or a girl? How do you feel about that? Are there things you wanted to try when you were a young child that you were discouraged from trying because of your gender?

★ Paikea's grandfather is loyal to the tribal traditions of his people. What are some family traditions that your parents and grandparents have passed on to you? What are some unique things your family does to celebrate holidays or birthdays that have special meaning to you?

★ When Paikea's father comes to visit, he asks her to consider moving to Germany and staying with him. She starts to leave, but then is called back by the ocean and says, "I have to go home." She considers her home to be on the land where she was born, with her grandparents, who have raised her. Where do you think of as your home? What makes that "home" to you? Who is there who makes you feel loved? If you have a birth parent who has not raised you, are there some things you would like to know about that parent? What questions would you like to ask her or him about the reasons you live with your adoptive family? What thoughts or feelings do you have about meeting that parent?

★ Paikea is a brave and determined young girl. At the end of the movie she plays a key role in saving the beached whales when she rides one out into the open ocean. What stories have you heard from parents or other relatives about brave or unexpected things you did when you were a child? What have you heard from your parents about what you were like as a small child?

★ Paikea's mother died while giving birth to her, and Paikea is being raised by her grandparents. What do you know about your own birth? On what day of the week were you born? What was the weather like? Where were you born? Have you been raised by the mother who gave birth to you? If you lost a parent at a young age, what do you know about that parent? What would you like to know?

★ In her speech at the school concert, Paikea speaks of her deep love and respect for her grandfather. She also acknowledges that she wasn't what her grandfather was expecting and that by being born, she broke the line back to the ancient ones. In what ways do you feel like you are not what your parents or grandparents were expecting? In what ways do you think you are more than what they were expecting?

★ Paikea has special insights and personal qualities that make her able to serve as a new leader and prophet for her people. What special qualities do you have that make you unique? What do you think is your "calling" in life? What kinds of people and activities are you drawn to?

Your Turn

Now it's your turn to write down any questions you would like to ask one or both of your parents about how you came to be their child and what makes you special to them. What do you *really* want to know?

_____

_____

_____

_____

_____

Activities

Parents: If you have a baby book that you kept during your child's infancy, pull it out and share it with your child. If you don't have a book, consider starting a memory journal. Write down what you remember about milestones in your child's first few years of life. For example, who was the first relative who held her after she was born, what was her first word, when did she take her first steps, how did you celebrate her first birthday?

Parents and Kids: Together, look through the family photo album. Kids, pick out six photos that were taken when you were a baby. Parents, for each picture tell your child the story that goes with the photo—when the photo was taken, where you were, who was there, what you were doing, how old he was, what time of year it was, and so on.

Kids: Go to www.dmarie.com/timecap and enter your birth date in the space provided, including the month, day, and year. Click on the "Quick Page" button. Print out the time capsule page. Have you ever heard any of the songs that were popular the year you were born? Have you seen any of the television shows? Ask your parent if he or she remembers the price of gasoline or a gallon of milk around the time you were born.

Parents and Kids: Separately write two lists. One list is "how to act like a boy" and the other is "how to act like a girl." Show your lists to each other. What are some things you agree on? What are some things you disagree about?

Parents of Adopted Children: If you haven't done so already, start developing a library of books for your child on the adoption experience, and let him or her know where the books are located and the information they contain. Ask your local librarian for help to find both fiction and nonfiction books that speak to both the facts and emotions of adoption.

Love Me Tender:
Support and Conflict Between Parent and Child

Chapter 5

Sample Questions Asked by Middle-School Kids ?

Do you love me and would you ever give me up?

Do you think I'm important?

What do you really think of me?

Can I have a hug?

If I get in trouble any time, will you tell me so I can correct my mistakes?

Why do you break me down inside and hurt me outside all the time?

Why don't you have any time for me?

Can we stay together forever?

Why don't parents talk openly with children if we talk openly with them?

Can I fall back to you if I have a problem?

⭐ A Few Things for Parents to Know

As your child moves into the preteen years, you may begin to notice some changes in your relationship with him. Do you find that you're spending less time in shared activities? Does it seem as though he would rather talk to his friends than you? Is he embarrassed if you try to kiss or hug him in front of other people? Are there days when it seems like whatever you say is the wrong thing? If so, you're not alone. All of these are typical of the changing relationship between parent and child during the middle-school years. Closeness decreases as parents and children spend less time together and kids choose to confide in friends more than in parents. Conflict increases as kids develop new reasoning skills that enable them to question their parents' rules and expectations.

It is likely that your middler also has noticed these changes in your relationship. The largest percentage and the most poignant questions kids asked in response to our research were about their relationship with their parents. Kids this age want to know how their parents feel about them. They want to feel accepted by their parents and to be able to talk about problems and issues in their lives. They're unhappy about having arguments with their parents, and they want to understand why some of those conflicts can turn so hurtful. This chapter offers you the chance to reflect on the relationship between you and your young person, acknowledge any areas of concern that you may want to tend to, and celebrate the love you share.

Human beings have an inherent need for acceptance. For most individuals the first and primary source of acceptance is the parent. Parents convey their acceptance in many different ways, for example, with their affection, care, comfort, concern, nurturance, and support. The expression of acceptance can be physical, verbal, or symbolic, but of primary importance is that it be reliable, consistent, and unconditional. More simply put, all children need to have at least one person who is absolutely head-over-heels crazy about them all the time and no matter what. Ideally that person is a parent.

When kids are infants and young children, most parents find it easy to feel affection towards them. Looking at their sweet faces while they're sleeping, or seeing them cry when they're upset pulls at our heartstrings. But as kids move into the preteen years, what came so

WHAT KIDS *REALLY* WANT TO ASK

easily before may now seem complicated. It can be difficult to look at a sulking preteen and feel an urge to hug her, or see the mess on her bedroom floor and be overcome with affection towards her. However, parents need to keep expressing love to their kids even when it seems nearly impossible to do.

Expressing affection is also so much easier with infants and young children compared to middlers. You can hold them, kiss them, sing to them, play with them. But when a child is in early adolescence, ways to express parental affection and acceptance may not be as obvious as they once were. He may not want you to tuck him in bed at night, he might shrink from your attempts to hug and kiss him, he might react with "yeah, whatever" in response to "I love you." But none of that means he no longer needs or wants your love. It just means that you have to find new ways to convey it. Expressions of love may become more symbolic, like setting rules to protect him from people or situations that might be dangerous, preparing his favorite breakfast on the day of a big math test, or sitting in the rain to watch him play a soccer game.

One of the most loving things you can do for your young person is to be available to listen and offer support when she has a problem. While she may confide in friends about some of her social issues, she will take comfort in having a parent as a soft place to land when she has upsets that friends can't help her with. And during the middle-school years, a child is likely to experience a lot of troubles, from finding out her latest "crush" doesn't return her feelings, to worrying about the newest pimple on her face, to forgetting to turn in her homework assignment. As trivial as some of those issues may seem to you as an adult, it's important to treat them as the meaningful concerns they are to your child. If you can respond with empathy and genuine concern to the small matters, she will be more likely to seek you out for help with any bigger, more serious matters that arise.

Of course there will also be many moments of happiness and joy in the life of your young adolescent. You can also show your love by sharing in his happiness and celebrating his successes. Setting aside time every day to hear about what's going on in his life lets him know you care. For many families this time might be the dinner hour. For others, it might be the last thirty minutes before bedtime or during the drive to school or other activities. Do you spend time talking with your middler every day? Do you know what's going on in his life? We recommend that you reread the section called "Communicating with Your Preteen" in the introduction of this book. In fact, you might want to refer to those pages every few weeks just to be sure you're doing everything you can to communicate your acceptance, support, and love for your young person. Building a strong foundation now will pay big dividends in a few short years.

The movie for this chapter illustrates what can happen in the absence of parental acceptance. Believing that parents do not really love or care about her can result in a host of psychological and social complications for a child. Personal insecurity, anxiety, anger, resentment, and depression all have been attributed to the absence of parental acceptance. If an individual feels her parents don't love her, she may in turn come to view herself as unlovable. She may close off emotionally and have difficulty expressing and receiving love. She may adopt a defensive approach in social relationships, expecting the worst from people and perceiving hostility where none is intended.

Most experts agree it's not the absence of affection per se, but rather the individual's perception of parental rejection that can be so devastating. So even if you think you're doing things to express your love and acceptance to your child, it's not how the message is sent but how it is received that matters. If you think you're expressing your love and acceptance to your child but he responds negatively, try asking him for feedback. Tell him, "I'm trying to let you know that I love you, but it doesn't seem to be working. What could I do that would work better for you?" It also might be helpful to ask someone who is privy to your private interactions to give you some objective feedback. What you think of as loving might really be transmitting an unloving message. For example, parents who seek to control a child may unintentionally project the message that he is untrustworthy or unable to handle things for himself. Spend some time reflecting on the messages you give your child in both words and deeds. What do you do to tell your middler you love him? Does he know that you think he is important? Kids need to hear dozens of "I love yous" for every harsh word they hear. How do you rate on this scale?

Conflicts and disagreements are bound to arise in any close relationship. The parent-child relationship during early adolescence is particularly vulnerable because kids have more advanced abilities to question their parents' rules and decisions and greater interest in spending time with friends away from parental control. Chances are most of the arguments that happen between you and your middler concern the "small stuff" of life like curfew, keeping her room clean, and how much time she's spending in front of the television or computer. The thing to be concerned about is not whether you argue, but how you argue. Are you prone to yelling and swearing? Do you lose your temper easily and say things you later regret? Or are you able to calmly and rationally express yourself using "I" messages and feelings? Do you spend so much time talking or venting about what's upsetting you that you don't give your young person a chance to express her point of view? Or do you try to find a compromise position so that both of you feel heard and can be satisfied with the outcome? Do you harbor grudges and refuse to take any responsibility for the disagreement? Or do you take the time to apologize afterwards and admit your part?

Hearing and seeing anger from a parent who is supposed to love him can be confusing to a young person and damage the trust he feels towards you. If you are prone to destructive ways of handling disagreements with your middler, consider seeking professional counseling to help you learn new ways to express your displeasure.

Another thing to consider is how loving and caring you are to other people in your life to whom your child is witness. Children learn much by watching you carry out other relationships, and they adjust their trust accordingly. Try to make it a habit to think before you speak and to follow the Golden Rule: treat others the way you would wish to be treated.

Most middlers and their parents value their relationships with one another and enjoy feeling close and connected. Kids may not act like they want hugs and kisses from you, but they do. It may not seem as though they're interested in family time and family talk, but they are. The movie *Smoke Signals* will give you a chance to have some deep

On With The Show!

Movie:	**Smoke Signals**
Year:	1998
Length:	1 hour 29 minutes
MPAA rating:	PG-13
Key actors:	Adam Beach as Victor Joseph
	Evan Adams as Thomas Builds-the-Fire
	Gary Farmer as Arnold Joseph
	Irene Bedard as Suzy Song
Director:	Chris Eyre

conversations with your middler about how much you love each other and to uncover some of the unspoken feelings between you.

Movie Synopsis

Smoke Signals is a drama that tells the story of Victor Joseph and Thomas Builds-the-Fire, two Native American young men from the Coeur d'Alene Indian Reservation. Thomas's parents died in a house fire when he was an infant, and Victor's father abandoned the family when Victor was 12 years old. When Victor learns of his father's death, he decides to travel to Phoenix to retrieve his father's pick-up truck and personal belongings. Thomas offers to pay for the bus trip, on the condition that he can come along. Throughout their six-day journey, Thomas reminisces about Victor's father and the ways he did and did not express love towards his son. The boys meet Suzy, the father's friend, who gives Victor more information about his dad. In the end, Victor comes to terms with his past and finds a way to forgive his father for the poor relationship they had.

Cautions

The movie begins with a house fire scene in which baby Thomas is thrown from a window to safety; no deaths are shown. Arnold Joseph is an alcoholic, and there are two scenes in which he is intoxicated. One occurs when Victor accidentally spills his father's bottle of beer as they are driving and Arnold hits him across the face. Later, during a drunken argument, Arnold hits his wife and then leaves in his pick-up truck. Swear words *(shit, bullshit)* are used a few times. Toward the end of the movie there is one flashback scene in which Suzy finds Arnold lying dead on his bed; he appears to be sleeping and there is no sign of trauma. Victor and Thomas are involved in an automobile accident near the end of the film, and a bloodied, injured woman is briefly shown lying on the ground.

Movie Talking Points for Parents

★ When Arnold (Victor's father) talks to his friend Suzy about abandoning his wife and son, he says the worst thing he ever did was "broke three hearts." What is the worst thing you ever did to cause emotional pain to someone you love? How did it change your relationship with that person?

★ Victor spent most of his adolescent and young adult years believing his father didn't love him. How do you express your love to your middler? What changes, if any, would you like to make in how you do this?

★ At the end of the movie, Victor realizes his father didn't really mean to leave. What are some hurtful things you have done to your child that you really didn't mean to do? When is the last time you said something hurtful to your child that you wish you hadn't said? What might happen if you said, "I'm sorry"? What makes that difficult for you?

★ Victor's father died before he had the chance to apologize to his son for all of the emotional pain he had caused. According to his friend Suzy, "He didn't want to die here, he wanted to go home." Is there any relationship in your life that you want to heal while there is still time? How important is it to you to forgive and be forgiven? What can you tell your young person about the process of healing through forgiveness?

★ Victor asks Suzy if his father ever talked about him. She says that he used to talk about playing basketball with Victor and that he was proud of Victor's basketball skills. What makes you proud of your young person? What are some of his accomplishments or abilities that you tell other people about? How often do you tell your middler you are proud of him?

★ Toward the end of the movie, Victor sees an image of his father helping him after the automobile accident. What are some ways you have helped and supported your young person through difficult situations or problems? What was meaningful about those times for you? How have those times been helpful to your middler?

★ Both Thomas and Suzy told Victor many stories about his father. They wanted Victor to remember the good things about his father instead of only the negatives. What are some of the good things you remember about your relationship with your parents when you were in early adolescence? What are some good things you hope your child will always remember about you? What do you do to create special memories with your child?

For Kids: What Do You Think?

Smoke Signals tells the story of a young man who was hurt and angry because his father didn't express much love towards him. Do you ever feel like your parents don't love and care about you? Are there times when you wish you could turn to your parents for support but feel you won't get it? Now is the time to talk about ways you don't feel loved and supported by a parent.

To help get the conversation started, share your answers to the following questions with your parent or parents and see what they say.

★ When Victor is deciding about traveling to Phoenix to claim his father's belongings, his mother says to him, "If you go, I want you to promise you'll come back." Can you think of a time when one of your parents said something to you that made you feel really important to them? What did they say?

★ Victor is angry because his dad abandoned the family when Victor was just 12 years old. How would you feel if your parent left you? In what ways do your parents let you know they are there for you when you need them? Has there ever been a time when you weren't sure? If so, what did they say or do that caused you to question their commitment to you?

★ Thomas's grandmother, who is loving and supportive, raised him. Likewise, Victor's mother is caring and loving. What things do your parents do or say that let you know they love you? How do you feel when they do or say these things? What are some things you wish they would do or say to let you know they love you?

★ As a young boy, Victor was very angry with his parents for their heavy drinking and their neglect of him. What kinds of things do your parents do or say that leave you feeling angry towards them? Do you ever feel that your parents don't love you? What do they do that leaves you feeling unloved?

★ Victor has fond memories of playing basketball with his father. What are some of your favorite memories of spending time with your parents? What are some of your favorite things to do with your mom? What are some of your favorite things to do with your dad? If you could have your mom or dad all to yourself for one whole day, what would you want to do together?

★ Toward the end of the movie, Victor feels comforted and relieved when he sees an image of his father helping him after the automobile accident. What have been some situations you have faced when a parent provided meaningful support and help? What makes it easy or difficult for you to turn to a parent for support? How do you feel about the amount of support and advice you receive from your parent?

★ At various points in the movie, Victor's mother, his friend Thomas, and his father's friend Suzy all try to get Victor to talk about his feelings towards his father. Victor gets irritated and is unable to express his feelings in words. How hard is it for you to talk about your feelings? Have you ever been able to tell your parents how you feel about them? What do you need from your parents that would make this easier for you?

✓ Your Turn

Now it's your turn to write down any questions you would like to ask one or both of your parents about the love, support, and conflict in your relationship with each other. What do you *really* want to know?

_____

_____

_____

_____

_____

_____

_____

_____

Activities

Parents and Kids: Play "Things I Love About You" around the dinner table. Each of you takes turns telling the other the reasons you love them. To make it more fun, try to alternate between silly reasons and serious reasons.

Parents and Kids: Once a month, plan a "Mom and me" or "Dad and me" day. Invite your child to make a list of activities he would most enjoy sharing with you. Then let him set the agenda for this special time each month.

Parents and Kids: Start a "Just Between Us" journal. Buy a blank journal or notebook and decorate the cover. Choose a place to keep the journal. Whenever either of you has something you want to discuss with the other that's hard to say out loud, write it down. It might be something you're angry about, or something you're worried about, or something you want to ask the other person. After you write in the journal, leave it on the other person's pillow. The other person can either respond in writing or make an appointment to talk about what was written in the journal. When you're finished with your discussion put the journal back in its keeping place until the next time one of you needs it.

Parents: Each day write *I love you* on a slip of paper and think of a new place to put the note (for example, in his shoe, in his coat pocket, taped to the bathroom mirror, taped to the television screen, inside a school book). Keep this up for as long as you can!

Parents and Kids: Practice "arguing by appointment." The next time you're upset about something the other person does or says, ask if you can schedule an appointment to discuss it. Make an appointment reminder card that says, "We have an appointment to discuss a problem on (day) at (time)." Before the scheduled time, write down your complaint using an "I" message format: for example, write *I feel ___[how you feel]___ when you ___[the thing he did or said]___*. Remember, there might be several feelings all jumbled up together. Try to state them all. For example, "I feel angry, confused, and frustrated when you tell me you'll be home at 6:00 and don't show up or even call until 8:00." During the appointment, read your statement to the other person. Try to follow a rule that each person must start every response with the word "I." See if you can remember to say, "I'm sorry," and offer a hug before the end of the discussion.

Parents and Kids: Create a "Good Times Memory Book." Spend an hour reminiscing about times you have spent together that have been fun, funny, or especially loving. Looking through photographs might help. Write down these stories in a notebook and add to it as new opportunities arise. Whenever you are feeling frustrated about something unpleasant that happened between the two of you, pull out the notebook and read through the happy memories.

Kids: Make a "Lend Me Your Ear" box. Whenever you have a problem you would like to talk about or a question you would like to ask your parents, write it down on a slip of paper and put it in the box. Talk to your parents about scheduling a monthly family meeting at which questions from the box are discussed.

Roots and Wings:
Trust and Responsibility Between Parent and Child

Chapter 6

> ### Sample Questions Asked by Middle-School Kids ?
>
> How come because I don't tell you what's going on in my life, you think I'm doing bad stuff?
>
> Can you totally trust me?
>
> Can I do anything I want?
>
> How come parents think they are always right?
>
> Why do you think grounding me will change anything?
>
> Why do you treat me like a little girl?
>
> Why are you so strict towards me?
>
> Why am I not allowed to swear?
>
> Why am I not allowed to go out and have fun?
>
> Could I go out on Fridays to get out, have fun, and socialize more with my friends and others?

★ A Few Things for Parents to Know

One of the greatest ongoing challenges of parenting is finding the balance between maintaining expectations for mature and responsible behavior and responding to your child's need for self-determination in an accepting and supportive way. It is a fact well established in research that children of parents who *find* this balance between "holding on" and "letting go" have the best outcomes. A significant number of the questions posed by middlers in the research had to do with issues involving trust and responsibility between themselves and their parent, especially on issues of the child's autonomy versus parental authority. Many of the questions started with *why* and included the word *allowed* as in, "Why am I not allowed to go out and have fun?" Kids wanted more freedom. Some expressed the ways they felt their parents were unfair to them or did not see them as individuals. Some indicated resistance to what they perceived as unjust or futile punishments. This is just as it should be! It is the job of teenagers to develop autonomy and to do so they must question their parents' authority. Most parents want their children to become independent, self-reliant individuals who can make their own decisions, take care of themselves, and lead productive lives. Remember, this is a normal passage that involves a great many changes and a lot of learning for both of you. Be easy with yourself and with your child and stay open to new ideas. What follows are a few perspectives informed by the writings of Alex Packer (*Bringing Up Parents*) and Laurence Steinberg (*Crossing Paths; You and Your Adolescent*).

Consider your own stage of development at this point in time. For many parents, their child's adolescence coincides with their own midlife struggles, so try to be honest with yourself about personal issues that may affect your attitude or behavior. While your preteen is dealing with the demands of puberty, you may be dealing with a body that doesn't work as well as it once did. Watching his seemingly endless energy may be a stark reminder of how yours is waning. As your child stands poised on the brink of his adulthood with a clean slate on which to write the choices he will make, your prior choices are an established fact. You may have regrets or a sense that time is running out for you. Overreacting to things that he's doing or saying is a clue that you might need to stop, take a breath, and consider what's really happening and why you're responding so strongly. It's possible that your own emotional issues are getting entangled with your reactions to your middler's behavior.

Recognizing your child as a separate individual complete with her own interests apart from yours will benefit you both. It will help her develop a sense of self-esteem based on her own unique strengths, and it will help you acknowledge the reality that children's lives are not meant to be duplicates of their parents'. The movie for this chapter, *Bend It Like Beckham*, portrays two families in which the parents (especially the mothers) have very definite ideas about what their daughters should be like, and seek to "mold" them to satisfy their own preferences. Do you see your role as a parent to be one of shaping your child by imposing your inclinations, or do you help her identify and develop her own natural interests? If she is attracted to something you consider frivolous, do you encourage her to explore it or discourage her because it seems like a waste of time? Helping your young person find her talents and passions can pay big dividends in terms of her self-esteem and happiness. Because we equate success in the teen years so closely with academic achievement, sometimes it's harder to notice and appreciate a talent if it does not fit the school venue. For example, perhaps your middler has the gift of making connections with people. Is she the social organizer who gets everyone on the same page to do something? Is she the mediator among her friends? Or perhaps your preteen exhibits prowess and passion for pastimes such as skateboarding or role-playing games? Identifying and encouraging the things she is good at helps her see and appreciate her strengths as well.

There are a lot of negative stereotypes about adolescents that can sometimes cloud a parent's judgment and interfere with seeing your child for who he is. These disparaging beliefs can make it easy to expect the worst from him rather than assuming the best. For over a hundred years adolescence has been labeled a time of "storm and stress" due entirely to the "raging hormones" of young people. Teenagers frequently receive bad press in this country and are often blamed for things that are in reality part of the adult culture. For example, although adolescents did not invent alcohol and drug abuse or early sexual behaviors leading to pregnancy and sexually transmitted diseases, the tone with which their involvement in these issues is reported in our media can make us believe they did. The fact is we are all constantly bombarded with conflicting messages about these things. It is adults who create those messages and adults who provide ample role models of dysfunctional behaviors for our young people to emulate. Humility is in order here. As you parent your middler on the cusp of adolescence, all the bad publicity about the teen years may lead you to think it is inevitable that he will "screw up" or disobey you.

A good rule of thumb, however, is to trust your child until you have a reason not to. Trust breeds trust. It also goes both ways. In the movie, the female protagonist lies to her parents and goes behind their backs to play soccer because she doesn't feel heard or seen as an individual. She feels she can't be open with them because their opinions are so strongly held, and she doesn't think they will ever change their minds. Work at developing a nonjudgmental, noncritical attitude; cultivate your curiosity about her life. And expect the best from her until she gives you some grounds for believing otherwise.

Frequently, it can be difficult for parents to decide when to exert authority and say "no" to a child's request and when to ease up and allow a child to make his own choice. In his book *You and Your Adolescent* Laurence Steinberg suggests that if an issue involves physical or emotional safety, standing firm and setting clear boundaries is the best course to take. However, if it has more to do with personal style, maybe a few more deep breaths and a private talk with another adult are in order! Between every parent and child there is a generation gap, especially about things like hairstyles, music, and clothing. Although you may find it difficult to understand why wearing pants that are about to fall down is desirable (using an example of a fad that may or may not still be in vogue), is it really harmful? After all, if the pants do fall, it's his problem and not yours; plus it may help change his mind about wearing them. Taking some time to figure out what it is specifically that bothers you can also be helpful. Are you remembering your own embarrassment about something that happened to you as a teenager? Do you hate wearing clothes that are constantly demanding your attention? Another approach is to be curious about what he finds attractive about the style. Does it help him fit in with a particular crowd at school? Does he see himself as a style-setting leader? Does it provide an identity or help him to be visible in the sea of students at school? While you're asking questions, you can also be sharing information about the styles from your generation and how your parents treated you, so he has a deeper understanding of where you're coming from. In like manner you may want to reconsider your approach to such things as hairstyle, room cleanliness, and other matters that commonly spark disagreement between parents and teens.

In striving towards that critical balance between providing roots and granting wings, it's important to distinguish between responsibility and privilege. A responsibility is an age-appropriate obligation for mature behavior, while a privilege is a right or benefit granted by a parent to a child. Work to confer early responsibility as your child becomes capable of handling it, and dole out privileges in stages based on her ability to manage the responsibilities linked to those privileges. For example, has she consistently demonstrated her ability to get home by the designated time? If so, you will probably be amenable to extending her curfew. If not, let her know the particulars of the responsible behavior you are using as the criteria to determine if she's ready for the privilege of a later curfew.

Let your child know that you won't make snap decisions about new things he wants to do, so that you have time to think things through. Also, develop a process in which he can work to alleviate your worries. For example, he wants to go to a concert in a nearby city. You are concerned because his plan is to drive with an older teenager you don't know and you suspect there might be pot smoking at the concert. There are legitimate concerns for his safety in this situation. But instead of giving him a flat "no," challenge him to allay your concerns by making a plan that you can live with. For example, he might convince a responsible parent to drive and to attend the concert. Or maybe you would be willing to do so in exchange for some work around the house. If he rises to the challenge, great! If he can't or won't make the needed effort, so be it. He may be disappointed, but you will both know that you were reasonable and he will see that you are not ignoring or dismissing his desires. As his ability grows to structure his activities so that you know he will be safe, your trust and, therefore, his privileges will also grow.

Finally, *Bend It Like Beckham* has a substantial subplot dealing with sexual orientation. This topic did not come up in the research on middlers' questions; however, this chapter provides a good opportunity for you to broach this important issue so your child knows you are comfortable doing so. For example, you could mention that Jules's mother thinks Jules is a lesbian based on a stereotype about athletic women, and ask your young person what she thinks about that. Or you can label the mom's behavior in the movie "homophobic" and explain what that means. Sexual orientation can be a divisive issue for families. Sometimes young people are punished for being honest about their natural tendencies. In addition, the suicide rate among homosexual youth is much higher than for youth in general. While some preteens might already know they are attracted to people of the same sex, most homosexual individuals do not report being "out" even to themselves at this age. However, as acceptance for homosexuals grows in our society, more and more teenagers are identifying their sexual orientation at earlier ages than in the past. If you are a gay or lesbian parent, the topic of sexual orientation might already be open for discussion in your home, but if you are a heterosexual parent, you may not have given the topic much thought at this point in your child's development. Do you expect you might be concerned if your son or daughter shows no interest in the opposite sex in high school? Do you believe sexual orientation is a choice or determined biologically? Do your religious beliefs include a strong stand against homosexuality? How will you respond to your child if she comes to you and says she's gay? This might be a good time to think through these issues and have a plan should the need arise.

As you and your middler tackle questions of trust and responsibility in your evolving relationship it is important to remember that, as mentioned in Chapter 5, your preteen wants closeness and acceptance from you even though he may act quite differently. Dispense love in liberal doses at every opportunity for your young person *and for yourself.* You're doing the hardest job there is!

On With The Show!

Movie:	**Bend It Like Beckham**
Year	2002
Length:	1 hour 52 minutes
MPAA rating:	PG-13
Key actors:	Parminder Nagra as Jesminder (Jess) Bhamra
	Keira Knightley as Juliette (Jules) Paxton
	Jonathan Rhys Meyers as Joe
	Anupam Kher as Mr. Bhamra
Director:	Gurinder Chadha

Movie Synopsis

Bend It Like Beckham is a contemporary film about an 18-year-old Asian Indian girl named Jess (short for Jesminder). Jess's family lives in

London, and she and her older sister, Pinky, were born there, but their parents immigrated from India. Jess has talent as a soccer player and plays pick-up games with the boys in the park, but her parents do not approve, due to some strongly held beliefs based on their generation and ethnic background. [Note: Soccer is called football everywhere except the United States, where football is a different sport.] A girl named Jules (short for Juliette) plays for a female team and encourages Jess to join. Jess secretly does so against her parents' wishes. She finds herself having to lie to do what she most loves because her parents don't understand how important soccer is to her. Jess's idol is David Beckham, a well-known soccer player, and her great desire in life is to have the ability to "bend it like Beckham." [Note: In 2007, Beckham began playing with Major League Soccer's Los Angeles Galaxy.]

 ## Cautions

It is difficult to understand some of the British and Indian accents in this movie, so you might want to rent the DVD and display the subtitles. Also there are a number of British colloquialisms used in the film that may be less familiar to U.S. viewers. For example, the phrase *over the moon* means "happy." There are some common English swear words like *bastard* and *bitch,* as well as British ones like *shag,* which refers to sexual intercourse. Several scenes involve girls changing their clothes in locker rooms, but no nudity is shown. Jules's mother jumps to conclusions about her daughter's sexual orientation based on an overheard conversation and the stereotype that girls who enjoy sports are lesbians. In addition, she makes several homophobic and stereotypical comments about lesbians; for example, "I bet your room at home doesn't look like this with all these great big butch women on the wall." There are also sexist comments made by young men about the girls playing soccer ("Check out the boobs on the captain"). Pinky (Jess's sister) is shown making out with her fiancé in a car, but they are fully clothed. Alcohol is being consumed at two clubs and at a wedding, but no one appears heavily intoxicated. None of the major characters smokes cigarettes, and drug use is not evident.

Movie Talking Points for Parents

★ More than anything else, Jess wants to play soccer and has a real talent for the sport. What do you recognize as a special talent in your young person? How do you encourage and support that talent? How do you discourage it? Why do you take the approach you do? When you were a teen, was there something you wanted to pursue that was discouraged by your parents? Looking back, what do you think of how they handled that? How would your life have been different if they had appreciated all of your interests?

★ When Jess tells her parents she's playing on an all-girls team and then says "he" to refer to her coach, her mother says, "See how she lies" before she has heard the complete story. Later, the parents of Pinky's fiancé think they see Jess kissing a boy at the bus stop and call off the wedding because they consider this shameful behavior. But Jess was with Jules and they weren't kissing. Describe a time when you or someone you know jumped to a conclusion about something a child did before he or she had a chance to explain the situation. How did you feel about that afterwards? How did the child feel? Has another adult ever told you something about your child that caused a dramatic stir but wasn't true? Did you believe them or check it out with your child?

★ Jess's mother is concerned about her skin becoming too dark because she thinks she won't attract a suitable husband. She also doesn't want Jess to show her legs or to be touched by boys. She thinks it's important for Jess to learn to cook a "full Punjabi dinner." These are all ideas based on her generation and her Indian culture. What strong opinions do you hold about the way your son or daughter behaves, and how is this related to your family of origin, the ethnic group to which you belong, or your generation? Do you have beliefs about what is appropriate for boys versus girls?

★ In one scene Jess's mom is teaching her to make a traditional Indian dish called Aloo Gobi, while Jess is practicing soccer moves with a head of lettuce. Towards the end of the movie, Jules's mother begins to pay attention to her soccer playing because she realizes, "I've got to take an interest or I'm going to lose you." In what ways are you and your young person different in your interests and talents? What are some interests and talents that you share? What are some of your child's interests that you don't know much about? What are some of your child's interests that you have learned about in order to stay connected?

★ Joe says to Jess, "Your parents don't always know what's best for you." Explain why you either agree or disagree with that statement.

★ Jess's mother recollects that her own mother chose all of the items in her dowry, while in contrast, she is allowing her daughter Pinky to choose her own. What are some ways you are less strict and give more freedom to your middler than your own parents did? If someone asked your child to name what matters you are too strict about, what do you think he would say?

★ Jess sneaks around to play soccer behind her parents' backs because she knows they wouldn't approve of her doing it. When you were young, did you ever sneak out of the house to do something you knew your parents wouldn't like? Did you ever lie to your parents about where you were or what you were doing? What is the biggest lie you ever told them? What happened when they found out? Have you ever caught your middler lying to you about something she did? How did you react to that?

★ The parents of Pinky's fiancé say at one point that "children are a map of their parents." In what ways do you expect your child's words and actions to reflect well on you? What are some things you push your child to do because of how it will make you look in others' eyes? How do you think your child feels about this?

★ Jess's mother is upset when she discovers that both of her daughters have been deceiving her. How important is it to you to be able to trust your middler to be honest about where she is going and what she is doing? What are some things you do to build that trust?

★ Jess's father's responses to her playing soccer are based on experiences he had when he was her age. First, he objects to her playing because he recalls the prejudice he confronted as an Indian who wanted to play soccer in England. Then by the end of the movie, he realizes he has been holding his daughter back and he decides, "I don't want her to make the same mistakes her father made of accepting life, accepting situations." What are some of your unpleasant memories from your teenage years? What are some things you do as a parent to try to prevent your child from having a similar experience? What are some of your favorite memories? Are there ways you push your young person to have some of those same pleasant experiences that you had? How do you think your child feels about this?

For Kids: What Do You Think?

Bend It Like Beckham is a movie that deals with issues of trust and responsibility between parents and children. Kids your age sometimes don't like the rules their parents have for them. This movie will help you talk about those things with your parents.

To get a conversation started about these important issues, share your answers to the following questions with your parent or parents and see what they say!

★ *Bend It Like Beckham* shows Jess talking to the poster of her idol, Beckham. Later in the movie, Joe says to Jess, "I don't talk to my dad because I know what he'd say." What (if anything) do you feel you can't talk to your parents about that is really important to you? What happened to make you feel that you couldn't talk about this topic? What topics do you avoid speaking about with your parents because their opinions are so strong they wouldn't be able to hear what you say? What would you like to change about this?

★ Jules's mother creates a scene at Pinky's wedding by accusing Jess and Jules of being lesbians. Has either your mom or your dad totally embarrassed you in front of other people? How would you like them to handle a similar situation in the future?

★ Jules's mom wants Jules to like boys, but her dad says, "If she's more interested in playing football [soccer] than chasing boys, well quite frankly, I'm over the moon about that." What are some ways your mom and your dad have different opinions about your interests and activities? What does your mom feel most strongly about? What does your dad feel most strongly about? Which parent is easier for you to discuss things with and why?

★ Jess desperately wants to play soccer, but her parents won't allow it because of family and cultural traditions. What are some things you would like to do that your parents don't allow? What reasons have they given for saying no? Do you think they are concerned about your safety? What could you tell them to help them understand why it is so important to you?

★ On the day of her sister's wedding, Jess is torn between doing what her family wants (staying at the wedding) and doing what she wants (playing in the final soccer game). Describe a time when you felt a conflict between wanting to please your parents and wanting to please yourself. What did you decide to do? Why did you make the choice you did?

★ Tony tells Jess, "What your parents don't know won't hurt." And

Jules says, "Just tell your mom you got a summer job." Have you ever lied to one of your parents? Why did you decide to lie? How would your parents have to be in order for you to trust that you could always tell them the truth?

★ Jess tells her soccer teammates that she can't marry a "goreh," or white boy, nor a black boy or a Muslim boy. She is expected to marry someone within her own ethnic group. She also is expected to learn how to cook a full Indian meal. What "rules" like this do your parents have for what they expect of you? Are there things you feel pushed to do by your parents that you're really not interested in? How do you feel about these "unspoken" rules?

★ Jess's sister Pinky sometimes helps Jess cover up her soccer activities and sometimes she doesn't. If you have a sibling, for what things can you count on his or her support? For what things would you never expect support?

★ Jess complains that boys never have to come home to help in the kitchen. And she and Jules both feel pressure from their mothers to behave more like young ladies instead of playing soccer. What are some ways you feel limited in your choices because you are a boy or a girl? What are some ways your parents' expectations for you are influenced by your gender?

✓ Your Turn

Now it's your turn to write down any questions you would like to ask one or both of your parents about trust and responsibility in your relationship. What do you *really* want to know?

_____

_____

_____

_____

_____

_____

_____

_____

_____

Activities

Parents: Make a list of "house rules." Include on the list things the kids are not allowed to do—things that are easy for parents to say "no" to, such as watching unlimited amounts of television, having friends over when parents are not home, swearing at parents. Then list things kids are expected to do—things that are easy for parents to say "yes" to, such as keeping your bedroom clean, washing dinner dishes, coming home by curfew. Now talk with your child about each rule on the list. Does it seem reasonable? Is it based on concerns about safety or deeply held family values? Is it a rule that would be negotiable and might change as kids get older?

Parents and Kids: Separately write a list of things you think the other person has a talent for. Then compare your lists and see if you agree with their assessment of your abilities.

Parents: Find a newspaper article in which a teenager has done something wrong or in which statistics about teenagers' unhealthy behaviors are provided. Read the article out loud at the dinner table and ask questions to get a discussion going with your preteen. For example, does the article mention the responsibility of parents or other adults in contributing to the problem? Does the article seem to imply that teens are more prone to unhealthy behaviors than adults? Does the article seem to suggest that this kind of behavior is "expected" of teens?

Kids: Make a list of things you look forward to doing for the first time in the next couple of years. For example, you might be interested in staying home alone on a Friday evening, going out on a date, going to a boy-girl party, going to a rock concert, staying up as late as you want to. Decide when you think you'll be ready to do each thing, and then have a discussion with your parents about the criteria they will use to grant their permission.

Kids: Think about the things your parents seem most worried about when it comes to you. For example, does your mom seem to worry more about physical injuries or hurt feelings? Does your dad worry more about your schoolwork or your performance as an athlete? Then, when things are calm, ask some questions to discover the experiences your parent had that might make him or her focus on those worries over others.

Parents: For one month, make a commitment to catch your child in the act of doing something right and to appreciate it out loud at least twice a day.

Parents: Is there something your child is interested in that you are not, for example, video or role-playing games, watching MTV, or listening to a particular band or type of music? If so, make a point to do some research about the activity on your own so you can ask intelligent questions about it. See if he would welcome you joining him in the activity a couple of times. This will help you gain a better understanding of his interest, allow you to speak more knowledgeably about what he enjoys, and transmit your acceptance of him as a separate person.

Everybody Needs a Friend: Peers and Friendships

Chapter 7

Sample Questions Asked by Middle-School Kids

Who was your best friend?

How many friends did you have when you were younger?

What does friendship mean to you?

How do you get people to like you for a friend?

How do you fit in with a group?

Could I have a friend come over?

What would you do if someone is bothering you?

Why don't all people keep secrets as good as I do?

Why doesn't anyone like me?

What is your opinion on my problems with friends and relationships?

A Few Things for Parents to Know

Take a few minutes and think back to when you were just starting middle school or junior high. Probably the students who attended your new school were from a number of different elementary schools. Suddenly you became a small fish in a much bigger pond. All the kids you had gotten to know through the previous five or six years were dispersed into the bigger group, and you may have found it difficult to make new friends as you struggled to navigate this larger social world. Can you remember anything specific about that time? Do you remember it mainly as fun or stressful? How did you get through it?

In the research for this book, kids' questions about friendships fell into two broad categories. They wanted to know about their parents' experience with friends as young people, and they also wanted help with difficulties in their own friendships or reassurance about their ability to have good friendships. While there weren't a lot of questions on this topic, what we know from our own experiences and from research is that peer relationships are one of the most significant issues for this age group. Social success in middle school is usually much more important to kids than academic success. Most children want to fit in with their peers and be viewed as "normal." This is easy to see just by noticing the similarity in the clothes they wear, the music they listen to, their hairstyles, and the types of activities they find amusing.

As your child moves into the preteen years you'll likely find that she is becoming interested in spending more time with friends and less time with the family. Interacting with peers allows your child to acquire and practice social skills that will serve her throughout her life. Time with peers also helps her to expand her self-understanding as she compares likes, dislikes, and personal insights with friends. So don't be overly restrictive about allowing her to spend time with friends. However, do make sure you know who her friends are and stay informed about what they have planned for their time together. Allowing her to invite a friend to join in on family activities or an occasional family mealtime can show your child that you respect and support her interest in social relationships and that time with friends doesn't have to come at the exclusion of family ties.

Young people are spending more time alone with their peers than they did in the past, and the influence of the peer group on adolescents is significant, especially in this age of rapid technological change. Often young people are learning and using new technologies at a faster rate than the adults around them and so must rely more on each other to keep pace. Speaking of new technologies, the widespread availability of cell phones, instant messaging, and chat rooms means that your young adolescent has almost unlimited access to peers. It also means that face-to-face interaction is less central to your child's peer relationships than it was to yours when you were a kid. Sharing one of the two movies in this chapter and discussing how things have changed provides an opportunity for you to understand your child's struggles with friendships more clearly.

This is also an opportunity for you to take some time to reflect on any difficulties you experienced with friends at that time in your life and to resurrect the feelings in order to clear them. Did you have a group of peers who liked to spend time with you, did you have just one special friend, or did you feel like a loner? Were you the target of unkind remarks or other forms of bullying, or did you engage in this behavior at the expense of others? If you are still holding emotion-laden events from that period, be aware that conversations with your preteen might be too heavy on the advice and not heavy enough on the empathic listening.

Another thing to reflect on when considering peer relationships for your child is whether he is more of an extravert or introvert. Although degrees of extraversion and introversion lie on a continuum, generally an extravert derives energy from spending time with people, while an introvert derives energy from spending time alone. Where are you on this continuum? How about your child? If you are more introverted, you may feel like your extraverted child is putting too much emphasis on social activities at the expense of more solitary pursuits. Conversely, if you tend towards the extravert end of the spectrum and he towards the introvert end, you may feel he is "failing" socially, although the amount of socializing he does could be just right for him. Or, he may feel he is failing as he compares his personality to yours. Providing him with some insight into the extravert/introvert personality may be reassuring. This is a good opportunity to support his individuality and unique gifts and interests, especially if he is finding it hard to be positive about himself.

Of course, there is sometimes a dark side to peer relationships, which can be expressed in the form of bullying. Bullying is equally prevalent for boys and girls but takes a different form for each gender. For boys it tends to be more overt and often involves punching, shoving, or other acts of physical aggression, or the threat of physical aggression. Girl bullying, called relational aggression, is more psychological in nature and plays out in body language, whispered comments, giving or withholding confidences, or playing one girl against another in a circle of friends. The result of bullying can be traumatic for the victim. Check in with your child about the bullying she experiences or witnesses. Providing information or sharing your experiences may be helpful to her as she builds her relationship muscles.

Children this age are sensitive to the gender roles assigned and reinforced by the culture and don't want to act outside of those roles. This can be especially problematic for girls who enjoy more traditionally masculine activities and/or like to hang out with boys, and for boys who enjoy more traditionally feminine activities and/or like to hang out with girls. For the most part, young adolescents tend to congregate in same-sex groups because boys and girls at this age are interested in different activities. Boys may orient much of their time around physical activities such as playing sports or video games, while girls will use much of their friend time for conversing. While their preference is to be with same-sex friends, your son or daughter will probably attend his or her first boy-girl party during middle school. Most likely the boys and girls will congregate in their own groups and spend little time interacting with each other, while surreptitiously checking out the other group. Preteens are only just beginning to find the opposite sex interesting.

Because preteen friendships and activities differ greatly between boys and girls, and because we anticipate that preteens will be more engaged with a movie about their own group, we are providing two movies for this chapter: *Stand by Me* for boys and their parents and *Now and Then* for girls and their parents. The questions provided to stimulate conversations are directed to the same-sex parent. If that parent is not participating in the movie-watching for whatever reason, simply adapt the questions appropriately. For example, a mother might watch *Stand by Me* with her son and afterwards talk about what she knows about his father's childhood friendships. Or a favorite uncle or male friend could watch the movie and answer the questions. Or mom could just talk about her own early friendships and comment on how they were similar or different from those portrayed in the movie.

On a daily basis, issues with peers can lead to stress and joy for your child. If you're able to establish open communication and show him that you understand the importance of his friends, he will more likely come to you to share what's going on. And, offering information about your own experience from those crucial middle-school years can be reassuring to him and a bonding experience for you both.

Movie Synopsis

The movie classic *Stand by Me* (see "On With The Show!" box on the next page) tells the tale of a memorable summer for four boys living in a small, rural town in Oregon. It opens with Gordie, one of the four, who is now an adult and is reflecting back on events from the summer of 1959 when he and his friends were 12 years old. The boys decide to set out through the woods in search of a boy their age who has been missing for several days. They confidently depart with minimal

Movie:	**Stand by Me**
Year:	1986
Length:	1 hour 29 minutes
MPAA rating:	R (see Cautions for explanation)
Key actors:	Richard Dreyfuss and Will Wheaton as Gordie Lachance
	River Phoenix as Chris Chambers
	Corey Feldman as Teddy Duchamp
	Jerry O'Connell as Vern Tessio
	John Cusack as Denny Lachance
Director:	Rob Reiner

supplies, hiking along the railroad tracks and through the woods. They experience a series of adventures along their way, including a close encounter with a junkyard dog, a near-miss with a locomotive, a leech attack when swimming in a muddy pool, and one scary night around a campfire. Their journey ends when they find the dead body of the missing boy and successfully confront some teenage hoodlums. Although parents are only briefly portrayed in the story, their presence is evoked in several emotional scenes between the boys. The distinct personalities and camaraderie of the four, as well as the challenging situations they encounter, provide a rich glimpse into the special world of young male relationships.

Cautions

Stand by Me is the only film in this book to have an R rating, but we think by today's standards it should be PG-13. There is a great deal of swearing throughout the film by the main characters (*damn, hell, shit, asshole, tits, faggot, fuck, dick, bitch*), but the language seems realistic in the context of 12-year-old boys of the time period. The boys frequently call each other *pussy* or refer to each other as girls in a derogatory way. They experiment with smoking cigarettes. A handgun plays a significant role in the story, although no one is harmed by it. The topic of death figures prominently in the story. At the beginning of the movie the adult narrator tells us that Chris (his best friend) was recently murdered. This event is what prompts him to reminisce about this special summer they shared. In the 1959 events, Gordie's brother has recently died; this combines with the boys' search for the missing 12-year-old and their discovery of the body—the first time any of them have confronted the possibility of their own deaths or the death of a friend.

Movie Talking Points for Parents

★ *Stand by Me* is set in 1959 rural Oregon. What year were you 12? Where did you live? What activities did you do that summer? Who were your best friends? Did you have one special friend, hang out with a group of friends, or did you spend a lot of time alone? If you spent time with friends, what activities did you do together? In what ways was your childhood different from the movie? Different from your son's childhood?

★ The four boys in *Stand by Me* seem to have a great deal of freedom. Their parents are barely shown in the movie, and being away from home overnight was easily accomplished. How does this level of freedom compare to your experience when you were 12 years old? How does it compare to the freedom your son experiences?

★ There are lots of things the boys do that are particular to the period of history portrayed in the movie; for example, pinky swear, "two for flinchin'," "give me some skin," mailbox baseball. What sayings or behaviors were common to you and your friends when you were young?

★ The four boys are loyal to each other. Was there ever a time that a friend stood by you in a tough situation, or abandoned you when you really needed him? What can you tell your son about being loyal and trustworthy?

★ Chris, Gordie, and Teddy pick on Vern at several points in this movie. Were you picked on as a boy? What can you share with your son about dealing with teasing or bullying among boys?

★ The four boys have really different personalities in *Stand by Me*. The narrator, Gordie, is a sensitive storyteller, reeling from the death of his brother and the rejection by his father. Chris, though sensitive as well, has been stereotyped as a tough guy and a loser in his community. Teddy is flamboyant, aggressive, and angry. Vern is a scaredy-cat and often picked on by the other boys, but his enthusiasm got the whole adventure started. In what ways were you like any of these boys when you were 12? Did you ever hang out with someone whose personality was really different from yours? What sort of personality does your son have; for example, is he more of an introvert (prefers spending time alone) or an extravert (prefers spending time with friends)? How does he see himself?

★ The boys are halfway across a huge railroad trestle when they realize a train is coming, and they barely get off alive. What was the scariest thing you ever did with your friends as a young person?

★ Gordie is struggling with the rejection of his father. Chris's dad is an alcoholic, and Teddy's dad severely abused him. Vern's older brother and friends are aggressively threatening to the younger boys. Did you ever witness one of your friends being abused by a parent or a sibling? How did that feel? What did you do?

★ The boys in the story discover the body of a boy who died at age 12.

Did you know anyone who died young when you were a preteen? What happened? Did you go to the funeral? What thoughts or feelings about death do you remember from that time?

★ What is your reaction to the final comment made by the narrator: "I never had any friends later on like the ones I had when I was 12"? What do you know about meaningful and enduring friendships? What qualities make a good friend?

For Kids: What Do You Think?

Stand by Me tells the story of four 12-year-old boys having an adventure in 1959 rural Oregon. Do you ever wonder about the kind of friends your dad had and the things he did with his friends when he was your age? Do you have concerns about your own friendships?

Here are a few questions to get an interesting conversation going about friends.

★ The boys in this movie seem to really like being together. Even though there are occasional fights, they stick together and take care of each other. Have you ever had an overnight adventure with friends? How did it compare to the movie?

★ Early in the movie Teddy plays chicken with a train and Chris pulls him off the tracks. Has a friend of yours ever stopped you from doing something risky? Have you ever stopped a friend from doing something risky? What do you think your dad would say if you told him about something risky you or a friend had done?

★ Do you think you are more like Gordie, Teddy, Chris, or Vern, or are you a combination of those characters or nothing like any of them? Which of these characters do you like the best? Which one reminds you of one of your friends?

★ The boys in the movie live in rural Oregon in 1959. The era and location in which your dad grew up was probably different from that and *really* different from how things are for you today. What issues with friends do you think your dad would have trouble dealing with if he were your age right now? What issues with friends do you think he would have an easier time handling than you do?

★ Chris and Gordie are such good friends they can share their sad feelings together and offer each other a shoulder to cry on. Which of your friends can you trust to share hard feelings with? Do any of your friends have abusive parents or siblings? How is it for you to know this about them?

★ The boys in *Stand by Me* have their own tree house where they hang out together. Where's your favorite place to hang out with your friends? What do you think is the biggest difference between the things you do with your friends and the things your dad might have done with his friends when he was young?

★ The boys in *Stand by Me* give two hits on the arm ("two for flinchin'") when they make a friend flinch, and say, "Give me some skin" when they want to make up after a fight. What things like that do you say or do to your friends?

★ Vern is teased a lot by the other three boys. Are you teased or bullied by other boys or girls? If so, how do you usually react? Is this something you'd like help with from your mom or dad or another adult? If so, what sort of help would you like? What boys at school would you most like to be friends with and which ones would you never want to be friends with? Why?

✓ Your Turn

Now it's your turn to write down any questions you would like to ask your dad or mom about friendships. What do you *really* want to know? (Use the lines at the top of the next page.)

On With The Show!
(for girls)

Movie:	**Now and Then**
Year:	1995
Length:	1 hour 40 minutes
MPAA rating:	PG-13
Key actors:	Christina Ricci and Rosie O'Donnell as Roberta
	Thora Birch and Melanie Griffith as Teeny
	Gaby Hoffmann and Demi Moore as Samantha
	Ashleigh Aston Moore and Rita Wilson as Chrissy
Director:	Leslie Linka Glatter

Movie Synopsis

Now and Then opens as three young adult women arrive to be with their friend Chrissy, who is about to deliver her first baby in the small Indiana town where they all grew up. The focus soon shifts from present day to the summer of 1970, when the four were 12 years old. Independent and creative, these best friends spend every waking moment together. Their main pursuit is trying to find out what happened to a boy named Johnny, whose headstone in the local cemetery reveals that he died at about their age. They are also collectively saving money to purchase a tree house kit for Chrissy's backyard. While pursuing these activities they discover and share things about themselves that move them toward maturity. Each of the girls has a distinct personality and the movie portrays an easy camaraderie, loyalty, and sensitivity among them. At the end we learn that their reunion as adults is the result of a solemn oath they made the year they were 12.

 Cautions

Sexuality is a major topic of conversation among the four girls in *Now and Then,* and their discussions seem realistic. The tomboy of the group (Roberta) does not want her breasts to develop and flattens them with tape every morning. Chrissy gets a sex lecture from her mother involving metaphors like gardens and hoses that leaves her more confused than ever. In one scene, the girls come upon their nemesis: four neighborhood boys skinny dipping in the local creek. The girls steal the boys' clothes and there is brief frontal nudity as the boys give chase. The scene is sensitively done and a grand introduction to male anatomy for pubescent girls. There is discussion of French kissing and "doing the deed" among the 12-year-olds. Viewers also witness the adult Chrissy delivering her baby at the end of the film, but nothing is shown below the waist. Additional scenes have the girls answering a sex survey in a magazine and Roberta sharing her first kiss with a boy. The topic of death is also prevalent. Samantha tries to retrieve a precious bracelet from a storm drain during a heavy downpour and nearly drowns (but is saved in the nick of time). One of the girls lost her mother at age 4 and discovers the truth about the accident in which her mother died. Sprinkled throughout the film are common swear words *(bitch, shit, damn it, asshole, fat ass)*. Three of the girls try their first cigarette and two of the adult women smoke.

Movie Talking Points for Parents

★ *Now and Then* is set in 1970 in a small suburban town in Indiana. What year were you 12 years old? Where did you live? What activities did you do that summer? Who were your best friends? Did you have one special friend, hang out with a group of friends, or did you spend a lot of time alone? If you spent time with friends, what sorts of adventures did you have together? In what ways was your childhood different from the movie? Different from your daughter's childhood?

★ The four girls in *Now and Then* seem to have a great deal of freedom. Their parents are barely shown in the movie and being away from home for a day-long excursion on bicycles was easily accomplished. How does this level of freedom compare to your experience when you were 12 years old? How does it compare to your daughter's freedom?

★ There are some things the girls did that were particular to the period of history portrayed in the movie; for example, playing the game "Truth or Dare" and taking a sex survey from a popular women's magazine. What things like this did you and your friends do when you were young?

★ The four girls are loyal to each other. Was there ever a time that a friend stood by you in a tough situation, or abandoned you when you really needed her? What can you tell your daughter about being loyal and trustworthy?

★ The girls in this movie tease each other a little bit but are never cruel to each other. Girlfriends *can* be cruel, however. Were any of your girlfriends bullies? Did you ever bully anyone? What advice can you give your daughter about dealing with girl bullying?

★ The four girls have really different personalities in *Now and Then*. The narrator, Samantha, is struggling with the divorce of her parents and as an adult seems cynical about life and love. Chrissy is enthusiastic and a bit naïve. Roberta is a tomboy and doesn't shy away from confrontations with boys. Teeny dreams of being a movie star. Were you like any of these girls when you were 12 years old? Did you ever hang out with someone whose personality was really different from yours? What sort of personality does your daughter have; for example, is she more of an introvert (prefers spending time alone) or an extravert (prefers spending time with friends)? How does she see herself?

★ Samantha has a scary, life-threatening experience as she tries to retrieve a bracelet from a storm drain. Teeny tries to help but can't. What was the scariest thing you ever did with your friends as a young person?

★ Samantha cries when she tells Teeny her parents are divorcing, and Roberta gets angry and smashes things when she finds out the truth about her mother's death. Did a close friend ever confide in you when you were young? In what ways were you able to be supportive to your friend? Was there something you wish you had done but didn't?

★ The girls in the story discover the grave of "Johnny" who died at age 12. Did you know anyone who died young when you were a preteen? What happened? Did you go to the funeral? What thoughts or feelings about death do you remember from that time?

★ The four girls in *Now and Then* are supportive and loyal to each other. What can you tell your daughter about meaningful and enduring friendships?

For Kids: What Do You Think?

Now and Then tells the story of four girls in a small Indiana town in 1970, during the summer they are 12 years old. Do you ever wonder about the kind of friends your mom had and the things she did with her friends when she was your age? Do you have concerns about your friendships?

Here are a few questions to get an interesting conversation going about friends.

★ The girls in this movie seem to really like being together. Even though there are occasional problems, they stick together and take care of each other. Have you ever had an adventure with your friends? How did it compare to the movie?

★ In the movie Samantha climbs into a storm drain during a heavy rain storm to retrieve a bracelet and Teeny can't pull her out. Has a friend of yours ever stopped you from doing something risky? Have you ever stopped a friend from doing something risky? What do you think your mom would say if you told her about something risky you or a friend had done?

★ Do you think you are more like Roberta, Chrissy, Samantha, or Teeny, or are you a combination of those characters or nothing like any of them? Which one of these characters do *you* like the best? Which one reminds you of one of your friends?

★ The girls in the movie live in a small Indiana town in 1970. The era and location in which your mom grew up was probably different from that and *really* different from how things are for you today. What issues with friends do you think your mom would have trouble dealing with if she were your age right now? What issues regarding friends do you think she would have an easier time handling than you do?

★ The girls in *Now and Then* finally save up enough money to buy their own tree house. Where's your favorite place to hang out with your friends? What do you think is the biggest difference between the things you do with your friends and the things your mom might have done with her friends when she was young?

★ The girls in *Now and Then* play "Truth or Dare." Do you sometimes play this game with your friends? What games, special expressions, or activities do you and your friends do together?

★ Chrissy gets teased a lot by the other three girls. Do you get teased or bullied by other boys or girls? If so, how do you usually react? Is this something you'd like help with from your mom or dad or another adult? What sort of help would you like? What girls at school would you most like to be friends with and which ones would you never want to be friends with? Why?

✓ Your Turn

Now it's your turn to write down any questions you would like to ask your mom or dad about friendships. What do you *really* want to know?

_____

_____

_____

_____

_____

_____

_____

_____

💡 Activities

Parents: As a gift to your child, start a special photo album where she can keep pictures of her friends and the activities they do together. Make a point of taking pictures for the album at every opportunity.

Parents and Kids: Each of you writes a list of the qualities of your best friend. Then you compare and discuss your lists. Is there anything you want to borrow from the other person's list and put on your own?

Parents: If possible, take your child on a trip to the place where you grew up or the house in which you lived when you were a preteen. Show her the places you used to hang out with friends, go to school, or the scene of some story you have shared with her.

Parents: Invite your child to look at family photographs or yearbooks from your middle-school years. Point out your friends and talk about their positive and negative qualities.

Kids: Get together with a friend or group of friends and, using a waterproof container of some sort, create a "time capsule" of items—photographs, letters, and other stuff—that best represent your friendship. Bury the time capsule in your backyard or hide it someplace where no one else will find it. Then plan a special date to dig it up, like the day you graduate from high school or the day when the first friend gets married.

Kids: Invite one or more friends over to plan the "best day ever." Where would you go? What would you do? Would it cost money? Would you need help from a parent?

Kids: Is there someone you've been wanting to start a friendship with but feel too shy to approach? If so, have a talk with your mom or dad about what they could do to help. Could you invite the person to a family outing? What about a movie?

What's Love Got to Do with It?
Romantic Relationships

Chapter 8

Sample Questions Asked by Middle-School Kids **?**

What age did you start dating?

At what age did you first kiss someone or have a serious relationship with them?

When was the first time you had sex?

Is sex a good thing or not?

How do you know that you like someone and that he likes you?

When you like a boy, should you tell him or not?

When can I date and go to boy-girl parties?

Would it be okay to dance with someone closely?

Why do people act different around their friends than around their boyfriend or girlfriend?

Did you ever think you would never find love?

A Few Things for Parents to Know

During the middle-school years, most kids begin to take a new interest in and seek the attention of peers who are members of the opposite sex, whereas previously these peers were avoided or at best tolerated. A small minority of preteens may experience attraction to same-sex peers, or to peers of both sexes. Since only a small percentage of gay adults report having identified their same-sex attraction in middle school, and published research on sexual minorities in early adolescence is nonexistent, this chapter focuses mostly on heterosexual behaviors, and the selected movie is about male-female romantic attraction.

Some of the budding of romantic interest during early adolescence has its origins in puberty, as both hormones and brain growth contribute to new desires and urges. Studies have found that fifth and sixth graders spend one to two hours per week thinking about the opposite sex, while seventh and eighth graders spend four to six hours per week. The questions collected from kids in the research reflect this growing interest in romance. Middle schoolers are discovering new interpersonal attractions and wondering whether and how to act on the accompanying feelings.

Do you remember your first "crush"? Do you remember how old you were? Who it was? You may have spent hours thinking about that person, imagining what it would be like to talk to him or her, dreaming about spending time together, believing with all your heart that the two of you were "made for each other." Chances are the object of your crush didn't know how you felt (or maybe, didn't even know you existed), and your feelings were probably not reciprocated. Most likely you never spoke directly to the object of your affection. All of this was normal when you were young and, of course, is still normal for kids today. Most people report having experienced their first crush at around age 10½. Crushes are generally harmless and, in fact, can be helpful because they allow the young adolescent to explore at a safe distance the possibilities of seeing himself in the new role of relationship partner.

About one out of three young adolescents will have a boyfriend or girlfriend before age 14. But you needn't be too alarmed if you hear through the grapevine that your own middler is "going out," or if she tells you about a friend who is "going with" someone. Youngsters this age are immature in their notions about dating and romance. Among the middle-school crowd, "going with" simply means that a couple has made public their feelings of attraction for each other. These are typically short-lived relationships of only a few weeks' duration and often involve friends as intermediaries, as in "Ask Michael to ask Chris if he likes Jessica." And while the pair may spend some time interacting at school, this is likely to consist mostly of passing notes in the hallway, sitting at the same or neighboring tables in the lunchroom, and walking together to the bus stop. Contact outside of school is usually limited to a few phone calls or instant messages.

During early adolescence, expectations about whether and when to date are socially determined, and there may be a great deal of variation from one middle school to another. In some schools, the social pressure to have a boyfriend or a girlfriend starts as early as fourth grade, while in others, pairing off may be avoided in favor of group activities until high school. As a parent, you may find it helpful to ask your middler what messages his peer group is sending about the necessity or value of establishing romantic relationships. You may also want to examine the explicit or implicit messages about dating you are sending to your middler. Are you directly encouraging him to pursue romantic attachments or indirectly passing on a message to that effect? If so, you may want to reconsider your position.

Research finds no evidence of any positive effects of exclusive, one-on-one dating during the teen years. In fact, having a boyfriend for girls is associated with lower school grades and test scores; it is thought that pursuing boyfriends distracts girls from schoolwork and leads them to downplay their academic abilities. Romantic involvement for girls is also associated with lower self-esteem, depression, body image problems, higher risk of teen pregnancy, and, later, dating violence. For both boys and girls, early and frequent dating also increases the likelihood of sexual activity. These outcomes are especially evident among young people who use dating relationships as a substitute for same-sex friendships. As a parent it's probably better to discourage your middler from exclusive, steady dating and establish some basic rules that prohibit one-on-one dating until her high-school years.

Of course, there is nothing wrong with boys and girls spending time together, and there are benefits to be gained. First and foremost, it can be fun. Additionally, it also gives kids a chance to explore their attractiveness and what qualities they possess that make them desirable to others. It also provides practice in learning how to talk to the opposite sex. But none of this requires an exclusive, steady dating relationship nor does it warrant giving up time with same-sex friends. Instead, encourage your youngster to spend time with groups of boys and girls. Offer to host a Friday night pizza party at your house, or drive a group of kids to the local movie theater. Boy-girl parties can be fun and harmless, provided there is at least one adult chaperone and adult-monitored activities are planned.

Meaningful attachments to romantic partners won't occur until later in adolescence. Even so, now, while your middler is just beginning to explore romantic feelings and is therefore interested in the topic like never before, can be a good time to talk about the qualities that comprise a mature relationship. You may want to let him know that a healthy relationship adds to and does not detract from who he is as an individual. It is a place where he can be honest about himself and his feelings and be respected for all of his qualities. A mature relationship is pleasurable and not burdensome, and he should like the way he is with that other person. Equally important is that he be comfortable and content being alone with himself. Depending on a relationship to make himself feel complete as a person is a sign of low self-esteem and makes him vulnerable to manipulation and pain.

In addition to conversations about romantic attraction, this chapter will give you a chance to broach the subject of how much and what types of physical contact you consider to be appropriate between kids of middle-school age. Most adults would agree that feelings of physical and romantic attraction are a wonderful part of being human; however, if you're like most parents, it's probably difficult to imagine your middler as a sexual being. But the reality is that puberty brings with it new feelings of physical desire, sexual attraction, and arousal. Helping her to feel comfortable with her body and to accept feelings of arousal as normal and appropriate can go a long way in developing a healthy attitude toward her sexuality. Being willing to hear and answer her questions about sexuality openly and honestly, whenever they occur, is the best way to facilitate this. Sexual activity encompasses a wide range of behaviors. While sexual intercourse is not widespread among the middle-school population, more than four in ten middlers report that they have experienced a romantic kiss. By age 15, up to one-third of boys and one-fourth of girls will have tried sexual intercourse, more often out of curiosity than due to any meaningful emotional connection. Young people who are physically more mature tend to have sex earlier than "late bloomers." Among the middle-school population, oral sex is as common as intercourse. As is the case for dating in general, kids' perceptions of peer group norms have the biggest influence on the sexual behaviors in which they will engage. Therefore, those who think peers are "making out" or having sex are more likely to experiment than those who think peers are not engaged in those activities.

Most young adolescents have difficulty talking with their parents about sex, but most *do* want to talk about it. If he can't talk to you or his other parent, he'll likely turn to his peers. And those peers are probably just as uninformed as he is about matters of the heart and sex. Teens who talk with their parents are less likely to initiate early sex, particularly when those conversations focus on the social and emotional implications of choosing to be sexually active. An effective strategy is to be approachable and available, and to avoid a heavy emphasis on your personal views about the morality of sex or a description of the mechanics of sex and how to prevent pregnancy. These are important topics, but it's likely that your middler has heard about some of this in school health classes. Try to expand the agenda by talking about the possible changes in his reputation or acceptance among his peers. Offer some adult insight into how a relationship changes when a sexual component is added. Talk about the emotional impact of choosing to be sexually intimate with another person. Point out the advantages of postponing sexual involvement until one is in a mature, mutually committed relationship. Perhaps this chapter will give you the opportunity you've been looking for to open the dialogue.

Our social consciousness has not expanded enough yet to fully accept and allow individuals who may be gay, lesbian, or bisexual to express their feelings of romantic attraction openly. Since a stigma against homosexuality exists, it is impossible to know how many young people of middle-school age would identify themselves as gay, lesbian, or bisexual in a culture of acceptance. As a parent, it is important to remember that we live in a society in which heterosexuality is assumed. Unless you belong to a sexual minority yourself or have a close relationship with someone who is gay, lesbian, or bisexual, you may have never considered the confusion, fear, and isolation of someone who is experiencing, for the first time, romantic feelings for a person of the same sex. As a caring parent who may someday discover your child to be homosexual, now is an appropriate time to begin preparing a safe environment for her to "come out" to you. One way to do this is to initiate family conversations that signal your acceptance of sexual minorities. Voicing your support for an upcoming referendum for gay rights or inviting a gay co-worker to dinner with her partner will send a message that you value all people, regardless of sexual orientation. If you already suspect that your son or daughter may be gay, there is educational information and support available through PFLAG (Parents, Families and Friends of Lesbians and Gays) on the Internet.

On With The Show!

Movie:	**The Man in the Moon**
Year	1991
Length:	1 hour 40 minutes
MPAA rating:	PG-13
Key actors:	Sam Waterston as Matthew Trant
	Tess Harper as Abigail Trant
	Reese Witherspoon as Dani Trant
	Jason London as Court Foster
Director:	Robert Mulligan

Movie Synopsis

Set in rural Louisiana in the summer of 1957, *The Man in the Moon* is a touching coming-of-age story centered on 14-year-old Danielle (Dani) Trant. While swimming in the river one day, Dani encounters 17-year-old Court Foster, who has moved to the long-vacant family farm next door with his recently widowed mother and two younger brothers. Dani's initial feelings of irritation towards Court soon turn to infatuation and fantasies of romance. Court likes Dani's high energy and fun-loving nature, and the two become frequent swimming companions. Although Dani dreams of true love, her hopes are dashed when Court meets her older sister, Maureen, and falls instantly in love with her. Conversations with her father and a tragic turn of events at the end of the movie expose Dani to new emotions and life lessons about love and loss and the abiding importance of family relationships.

Cautions

A few swear words (*ass, butt*) are used near the beginning of the story. Dani swims naked in the river, but no nudity is actually shown.

When Maureen goes on a date with her boyfriend, Billy, his father makes inappropriate advances towards her, but she effectively distances herself from him. Billy tries to force himself on Maureen in the front seat of his car; when she resists and clearly tells him "no," he gets angry and drives her home. The movie contains a few depictions of physical affection. Court gives Dani her first kiss, but it is not at all erotic. Later Court kisses Maureen with great tenderness and affection. This is followed by a scene showing Court and Maureen lying amidst a cluster of trees, passionately embracing and kissing with clothes off; it is a tasteful depiction of tender love. There is one scene involving harsh physical punishment when Dani's father hits her with his belt for being out at night in the rainstorm, although the viewer doesn't actually witness the act. Later, Dad makes a sincere apology and they hug. There are two scenes involving blood. One occurs midway through the movie when Dani's mother falls and hits her head while running to find her daughter during a rainstorm. Toward the end of the movie, Court is killed in a tractor accident. Only the immediate aftermath of the accident is shown, when Dani happens upon the sight of Court's mother cradling his bloodied body.

Movie Talking Points for Parents

★ In speaking about her husband, Abigail recalls, "I had a crush on him since I was 13; he was 17 and didn't even know I was alive." Who was your first crush? How old were you at the time? Did you ever talk to or spend time with that person? How did the crush end? Whatever became of that person?

★ Near the beginning of the movie, Maureen's boyfriend, Billy Sanders, tries to manipulate her into a physical relationship with him. Billy's father also makes inappropriate advances towards her. In contrast, Court is sensitive and respectful in his expressions of affection toward Maureen. What do you consider to be appropriate ways for a man to express his affection toward a woman? What can you tell your young person about how to treat a boyfriend or girlfriend with respect? What advice can you offer about what to do when treated disrespectfully?

★ When Maureen leaves for her date with Billy Sanders, Abigail reassures Matthew, "She'll be fine." Dad is nervous, however, because, "I remember his father at his age." How do you feel about the prospect of your middler starting to date? What will be difficult about letting him or her go out with someone for the first time? What will be easy about it? What do you remember about your own experience that makes it easier or harder to imagine your child dating?

★ When Maureen goes to a dance, her father gives her date a clear message about her curfew. When Dani is interested in Court, her father tells her, "You're too young to date. If you want to see that boy, bring him over here to the house." At what age will you allow your son or daughter to date? Will you expect to meet the boy or the girl before the date? What curfew will you set? Would you have the same rules for a daughter as for a son?

★ Dani asks Maureen about kissing a boy. Court gives Dani her first kiss. Do you remember your first kiss? What did it feel like? How old were you? Where were you when it happened? Did you enjoy it or were you too nervous? How did you learn to kiss? Who could you ask about romantic or sexual matters when you were young?

★ Maureen and Court experience an immediate attraction, and both of them have intense, passionate feelings for the other. Do you think love at first sight can last a lifetime? If you have a partner, how would you describe your feelings for him or her at the beginning of your relationship? How are your feelings for each other now? What advice about romantic relationships do you wish you had been given (or had listened to) as a young person?

* Near the end of the movie, Dani's father says that "part of loving means risking the loss of that love." What would you say are the joys or benefits of loving someone? The risks or downsides? What adjectives would you use to explain romantic love to your middler?

* Shortly after they fall in love, Court and Maureen engage in physical affection that includes some sexual activity. What kinds of physical contact do you think are acceptable between boys and girls who are dating? Does "being in love" make certain behaviors more acceptable? At what age do you think it is acceptable to hold hands? To kiss? To engage in sexual activity?

For Kids: What Do You Think?

The Man in the Moon tells a sweet story about Dani Trant, who falls in love for the first time and is heart-broken when the boy she has a crush on is taken away from her. How much do you know about dating and romance? Have your parents ever talked to you about what it feels like to fall in love? Now is the time to ask any questions you have.

To get your creative juices flowing, share your answers to the following questions with your parent or parents and see what they say!

* When talking to her sister about Billy Sanders, Maureen tells Dani, "I don't 'go' with him, I 'go out' with him." In response, Dani says, "Big difference." What do the expressions *going with* and *going out with* mean to you? Are these expressions still used or are there others that are more common? Is there a difference between the two? What kinds of things do kids your age do when they are "going with" or "going out with" someone? At what age do most kids start "going" together? Do you ever feel pressured to have a boyfriend or a girlfriend?

* As she is having new feelings about boys and love, Dani finds it helpful to talk to her sister about romance, kissing, and growing up. Do you have someone you can talk to about these topics? What are

some ways talking about them has been helpful to you? What have you learned from talking to other people?

★ Dani tells her sister, "I think love should be beautiful and powerful. I want to be swept away by it." What is your definition of love? Have you ever been in love? What do you think it feels like? Do you think it's possible for kids your age to experience true love?

★ Dani asks Maureen, "Have you ever liked somebody so much it almost makes you sick? My stomach ties up in knots and I can't breathe and sometimes I think I'm going to throw up." Have you ever had that butterflies-in-the-stomach feeling about someone? Did you tell that person how you felt? If not, what stopped you? How long did that feeling last?

★ Dani has much stronger feelings for Court than he has for her. She is disappointed when he won't kiss her and he says he just wants to be friends. Have you ever really liked someone who only wanted to be your friend? How did that feel? Are you still friends? What is the difference between being friends with someone and dating someone?

★ Dani is really jealous when she discovers that Court loves her sister, Maureen, and not her. She feels angry towards her sister. Have you ever had a crush on someone who ended up liking one of your friends instead of you? How did you feel about that? Did you and your friend get mad at each other because of it?

★ Dani is open about her feelings for Court, but he has difficulty being honest with her about his feelings for Maureen. Do you think it is a good idea to tell someone honestly how you feel about them? How comfortable are you talking about your feelings towards another person? Have you ever told someone you like them? What is difficult about doing that?

★ When Maureen goes out with Billy, he tries to pressure her into having sex; Billy's father also acts inappropriately towards Maureen.

Is there anyone in your life who is doing or saying things to you that make you uncomfortable or scared in his or her presence? Have you talked to an adult about that? What kind of help would you like with this situation?

✓ Your Turn

Now it's your turn to write down any questions you would like to ask one or both of your parents about romantic love and relationships. What do you *really* want to know?

_____

_____

_____

_____

_____

_____

Activities

Parents and Kids: Some ideas and traditions about dating and romance change from one generation to the next, and some stay the same. Discuss the terms listed below, and compare what's different and what's the same for your two generations. For example, is the phrase used by your generation? What does the term mean to you?

* Going together
* Going out
* Going steady
* Dating
* Making out
* Hooking up

Parents: Make a list of "House Rules for Dating" to use when your middler begins spending romantic time with someone. Among the important things to include on your list are the following:

* Age at which your child will be allowed to attend a party with both boys and girls.

* Age at which your child will be allowed to go out on a date (for example, to a movie) with just one person of the opposite sex.

* What will be your rule about meeting your child's dating partner before they go out?

* What will be your rule about meeting the parents of your child's dating partner before they go out?

* How many nights per week will your child be allowed to go out on a date?

* Will you allow your child to go out on a date on weeknights or only on weekends?

* Will you allow your child to have a friend of the opposite sex come over to your house when no adult is home (for example, during the afternoon after school)?

* Will you allow your child to have a friend of the opposite sex come over to your house when you are home?

* Will you allow your child to have a friend of the opposite sex go into your child's bedroom to play computer games or watch TV?

* When your child goes out on a date, what time will you expect them to be home?

* When your child has a dating partner visiting at your home, how late at night will that friend be allowed to stay?

Parents and Kids: Make a list of "25 Ways to Tell Someone 'No!'" Take turns thinking of ways to say "no" to someone who wants to date you, or hold your hand, or kiss you. Include the words you could use (for example, "I said *no* and I meant it") and actions you could take (for example, turning your back and walking away). Have the kids practice saying or doing each of these.

Parents and Kids: Take turns thinking of fun activities to do with friends other than watching TV or movies; for example, play miniature golf, build a snowman in the winter, go bowling, swim, or go sledding. See how many different ideas you can think of. Write your ideas on a list, and every time you plan to get together with either a group or just one other friend, choose something off the list to do.

Parents and Kids: Together, make a list of ways to express affection for someone without getting physical. Include both serious and silly ideas on your list; for example, call them on the phone and sing a love song, wink at them from across the room.

Parents: Go to the website www.talkingwithkids.org/sex.html and read the suggestions for how to talk to your kids about sex. Then go to www.teenpregnancy.org and click on the Parents link. Read the "10 tips for parents to help their children avoid teen pregnancy."

Parents and Kids: Kids, tell your parent all the reasons you can think of why kids your age want to have boyfriends or girlfriends. Parents, listen as though you are back in middle school. Talk about which of the reasons sound familiar to you and why.

Making the Grade: School

Chapter 9

Sample Questions Asked by Middle-School Kids

How was school when you were a kid?

What were you like in school?

Why didn't you go to college?

How would you feel if I got kicked out of school?

If I would flunk, what would you do? Would you help me or let me flunk again?

Do you think I am doing good in school?

Why do most kids hate school?

Why is it so important to you that I get good grades, stay in school, and don't do drugs?

Why do we have to go to school for twelve grades?

Will you help me with my homework?

⭐ A Few Things for Parents to Know

Do you recall your child's excitement on the first day of kindergarten? Do you remember him coming home each day eager to tell you what he learned and how much he liked his teacher? Now fast forward to the present. If your middler is like most kids his age, that earlier enthusiasm for school is rapidly disappearing. Most middle schools are larger and less personal than elementary schools, and the academic expectations are higher. Classroom lessons are geared more to seat-based learning, which appeals more to students who have stronger verbal and mathematical intelligence and compliant personalities. While your young person probably enjoys the active, socially oriented classes and experiences, such as physical education, music, and lunchtime, it's likely that in some of his academic subjects, he frequently feels bored and wants to "tune out." School work is the most common source of negative emotions, such as worry, boredom, and frustration, for young adolescents. Some of the kids' questions listed above reflect this reduced enthusiasm for school. This chapter will give you a chance to find out how *your* middler feels about school and to reflect on your role in supporting his education.

Between the mid-1800s and the 1920s all fifty states passed compulsory education laws requiring children to be enrolled in school from as early as age 5 until at least 16, depending on the state. If you're like most parents, you probably value education and want your children to do well in school. There is nearly universal agreement in our society that education is important: it helps protect against unemployment, it leads to higher wages and income, and it opens the door to jobs with opportunities for advancement. The amount of education a person attains is also associated with better health and higher social and emotional well-being as an adult. In short, getting a good education is considered an essential part of growing up, and for most children that means attending school for 180 days out of every year.

While the majority of children are enrolled in public or private schools, more than one million children in the United States are homeschooled, and the trend is growing. In about one-third of these cases, parents have chosen to keep their children at home out of concerns about the school environment, particularly in the area of physical and social safety. A similar number choose homeschooling out of a desire to teach their children religious and moral lessons. In some cases, homeschooling is chosen in response to what parents view as inadequate academic instruction available in the traditional school setting, or a disregard for children as unique individuals. Some homeschooling parents find traditional public schooling detrimental to their child's natural curiosity and desire to learn. If you have chosen homeschooling for your child, the content of this chapter could also lead to interesting conversations about your outlook on schools and learning. It also might help you uncover any concerns or desires that your child is not voicing about being homeschooled.

In addition to homeschooling, the number of public and private alternative schools and charter schools is on the rise. Such schools are meant to address needs that traditional public education might neglect. These schools lie on a continuum from back-to-basics, which emphasize traditional academic subjects, to schools where students design their own learning experiences and have a voice in making and enforcing rules and policy. These alternate educational opportunities may be especially appropriate for children who exhibit stronger spatial, kinesthetic (movement), self-reflective, interpersonal, or musical intelligence than verbal or mathematical intelligence. One interesting conversation you could have with your child could be started with the question "If you were in charge of designing a middle school and could have it any way you wanted, what would it be like and what would students learn there?"

Another engaging topic idea that signals your willingness to discuss school on a deeper level is to bring up what schools *do not* teach children. For example, most schools do not invest a great deal of time or energy in providing comprehensive sexuality education, conflict management skills, or interpersonal skills, yet these subjects are critical to each individual's quality of life. Most adults and children would probably cite their relationships as the most meaningful aspect of their lives, yet young people are given little help in developing effective skills in that area. How did the emphasis on academic learning over the development of social and interpersonal skills impact your life? How is it impacting your child's life? With 20/20 hindsight, what did you learn in school that was really valuable to you? What would you have changed about your middle-school and high-school experiences?

Approximately one out of ten young people do not complete high school. For most such individuals, the precursors to leaving school before graduation become apparent during the middle-school years. Factors such as a learning style that doesn't match traditional methods of instruction, trouble with teachers, and poor grades can result in young people feeling disconnected from school and can contribute to their decision to leave. Difficulties such as ADD/ADHD, lack of home support, unaddressed behavioral and emotional issues, and alienation from the peer group all impact the ability of students to focus and concentrate in a school setting.

While most middlers still recognize that graduating from high school is important, they may increasingly struggle with seeing the relevance of their academic lessons. "How will memorizing the names of the ancient Greek and Roman gods and goddesses be important for my adult life?" "Why do I have to know the quadratic equation?" As a parent, it's helpful to empathize with your child when she wonders about the meaningfulness of what she is learning or when she complains that her schoolwork is difficult or uninteresting. At times, it may be so. School experiences are not always structured in such a way as to allow for the great diversity of interests that young people have. You may want to let her know that you understand that school does not always seem relevant, but because school completion is strongly linked to future educational and employment opportunities, it is best to stick with it and do her best.

There are other good reasons to stay in school. In addition to being exposed to the academic subjects deemed essential, school is also a good place to develop personal behaviors that will support any future path your child decides to take. For example, completing assignments, turning them in when due, and organizing one's time well are all important things your child can learn in school, which will apply to anything he wants to accomplish as an adult. Setting a goal and applying one's abilities and persistence to reach it develops self-discipline. Self-esteem and self-confidence can grow from experiencing progress in school performance. The middle- and high-school years are also a time when a young person can be free to explore a variety of subjects and pursue extracurricular activities to help him discover what he's good at or what he really enjoys doing. Particularly within a public school setting, having the opportunity to interact with peers from a variety of cultural and family backgrounds and with a variety of academic and extracurricular strengths can instill an awareness and appreciation of human diversity. So, in addition to what he is graded on, a host of other learning is taking place that adds to the value of compulsory education.

The kids in our research wanted to ask parents for help with homework and wanted to know whether parents would offer assistance if they were failing a class. It's a well-established fact that parental involvement is the single strongest influence on children's engagement with and success in school. Offer help with the lessons or subjects that don't come as easily to your middle schooler; and if they don't come easily to you either, look for an outside source, such as a tutoring program or a relative or friend who can assist.

Your involvement needn't be limited to helping with challenging homework assignments, however. Setting and expressing realistic expectations for your middler is also key. Expecting perfection can set her up for failure and take the pleasure out of learning. It's important to acknowledge that not every young person is a straight-A student. Equally important is to expect your child to give her best effort and work up to her full potential. Help her establish future aspirations for herself; notice what subjects your young person enjoys and succeeds in, and express your enthusiasm and support for those. Your discussion about expectations and aspirations may lead to some questions from your middler about your own educational history. If school was difficult for you or if you never completed the education you had hoped for, now is the time to be honest about that.

It also may be helpful to structure your home environment to encourage commitment to school and learning. Monitor your young person's schedule and make sure he's not so overloaded with extracurricular activities that he doesn't have time for homework. A good rule of thumb might be to limit him to no more than two activities at a time. Even if he's not participating in structured outside activities, he may be using his leisure time in ways that interfere with school performance. On average, students in the United States spend over 6 hours per day in front of computer, television, or videogame screens while the average amount of time spent reading on a daily basis is less than an hour. If this describes your preteen, you may want to consider limiting screen time; removing the television and computer from his bedroom may be called for.

If your child is being educated in a traditional school setting, communicating with her teachers and other school personnel is a critical component of her education. If your young person has multiple teachers, the prospect of meeting and consulting with them may seem more daunting than it was when she was in elementary school, so taking advantage of opportunities like an open house and parent-teacher conferences is a good way to meet these important people in her life. Having established some initial contact will be particularly important if and when a problem arises with her school behavior or grades. Most middle-school teachers would prefer to work in partnership with a student's parents to resolve challenges and to celebrate successes.

Early adolescence has been referred to as a turning point in young people's educational development. It is a time when the brain is ripe for learning and the doors to future paths are wide open. It is a time when a passion for learning can be ignited or extinguished. As a parent you have an important role to play in helping your child make the most of his or her educational potential.

On With The Show!

Movie:	**Akeelah and the Bee**
Year:	2006
Length:	1 hour 52 minutes
MPAA rating:	PG
Key actors:	Laurence Fishburne as Dr. Joshua Larabee
	Keke Palmer as Akeelah Anderson
	Angela Bassett as Tanya Anderson
Director:	Doug Atchison

Movie Synopsis

Akeelah and the Bee tells the delightful story of 11-year-old Akeelah Anderson, who discovers an aptitude and a passion for spelling. She is a bright girl who is teased by her peers for being a "brainiac," and because of the teasing, she doesn't apply herself at school. Her mother, appreciating the value of a good education, is insistent that Akeelah should concentrate on her schoolwork but is too busy with her job and family responsibilities to provide assistance. Under pressure from the school principal, Akeelah reluctantly enters the school spelling bee, and her success leads to a new-found ambition to compete at the regional, the state, and eventually the national levels. Along the way she forges new friendships with several fellow competitors; builds a relationship with Dr. Larabee, a university professor who serves as a mentor and tutor; and rallies the support of her family and community to assist her in fulfilling her dream. For young and old alike, the movie delivers an important message about the web of support provided by family, friends, and community, and the integral role it can play in promoting student achievement.

Cautions

Few cautions are needed for this family-friendly movie. At one point, the word *ass* is used, but other than that there is no swearing. Akeelah's sister is a young single mother and one of her brothers is involved with a street gang. No sex, violence, or drug use is portrayed.

Movie Talking Points for Parents

★ Akeelah not only discovers that she is good at spelling, but she finds that participating in spelling bees is challenging and exciting. What activities at school did you find most enjoyable? What activities does your child especially excel in or enjoy? How do you support your child's involvement in these activities?

★ Akeelah's mother is too busy earning a living and keeping Akeelah's brother under control to notice Akeelah's accomplishments in spelling. She does, however, pay attention to the letters reporting the lapses in Akeelah's school performance. Have there ever been times when you have been too busy with other things to attend to your child's successes? Which do you notice and discuss more with your middler—the school assignments on which she does well or the assignments on which she does poorly?

★ Akeelah's mother wants her to succeed in school and insists that Akeelah attend summer school to make up for the poor grades she received. How important is it to you that your middler do well in school? What does *doing well* mean to you? Are grades of primary importance to you, or are there other ways you gauge your child's performance?

★ Dr. Larabee shows Akeelah an inspirational quote and asks her what it means. She says, "It means I'm not supposed to be afraid of me." Are there any quotes that you consider inspirational or meaningful in your life? What is the message contained in these quotes? Which of these would you want to share with your young person?

★ Akeelah's mother tells her that she dropped out of college because she felt out of place. Now, as an adult, she regrets that decision. How challenging was school for you? How many years of education did you complete? Do you ever wish you could do more? If so, what stops you from doing that now?

★ As Akeelah prepares to compete in the national spelling bee, she rallies the support of friends, neighbors, and community members to help her prepare. The entire community wants her to do well. What are some benefits to society of children being educated? Why do you think it was important for Akeelah's neighbors that she succeed? Who in your child's life besides you cares that he succeed in school?

★ It is really important to Akeelah for her mother to take an interest in and support her spelling. What do you do on a day-to-day basis to offer support to your middler?

★ As the date of the national spelling bee approaches, Akeelah finds herself growing weary from the hours of studying and the constant focus on preparing for the bee. She asks, "Why can't we have fun?" What do you do outside of work and school to relax and have fun with your middler?

For Kids: What Do You Think?

Akeelah and the Bee tells the story of a girl who dislikes school but loves words and studies hard to win the opportunity to compete in the national spelling bee. She discovers that support from family and community matters for success. How meaningful is school in your life? How important is it to your parents that you do well in school? Now is the time to have a deeper conversation about school.

To get your creative juices flowing, share your answers to the following questions and see what they say.

★ Some of the spelling bee contestants had parents who were pushing their children to win. Do you ever feel too much pressure from one of your parents to do well in school? How do you feel when your parents push you to earn good grades?

★ Akeelah asks her mother to come and watch her in the district spelling bee, but her mother does not attend. What does it mean to you to have a parent who cares about and supports your school success? Do you ever wish your parent would be more involved?

★ Akeelah is teased by kids at school for being too smart. What kind of pressure is there in your school not to be too smart? Does this ever hold you back from doing your best in school?

★ After she wins the first spelling bee, Akeelah begins studying spelling with other kids and discovers that support from friends can help her be successful. How do your friends motivate you to want to do well in school? How do they hinder your success in school?

★ Akeelah tells her mother that she hates Crenshaw Middle School and that nobody there cares. Do you enjoy school? What do you enjoy about it? Do you feel challenged at your school? Do you think kids at your school care about doing well? Do you think the teachers and staff care about the students?

★ When Dr. Larabee asks her what her goals are, Akeelah replies, "All I'm good at is spelling." What do you most like to do? What are your goals? How might school help you to achieve those goals? What school subjects or activities are most interesting to you?

★ Even though Akeelah's mother is not able to be very supportive of her spelling bee pursuits, there are many other adults who encourage Akeelah and contribute to her success. Who are the adults in your life who encourage you in the things you are interested in pursuing? How do they make a difference to you?

✓ Your Turn

Now it's your turn to write down any questions you would like to ask your mom or dad about school. What do you *really* want to know?

_____

_____

_____

_____

_____

Activities

Kids: Ask each of your teachers to tell you one quote that they consider inspirational. Go to www.wisdomquotes.com and find a quote you like about learning or success. Write these quotes on the front of your notebooks or hang them inside your locker.

Kids: Make a list of all the people in your life who care about your school success or who have contributed to your school success. Write a short note to each one thanking them for being interested in your learning and either e-mail, mail, or deliver the notes.

Parents and Kids: If there is someone in your extended family or group of friends who dropped out of high school, ask them to tell you how that decision has affected their life. Ask them if they would make the same decision if they had a chance to go back and do things over again. If there is someone in your extended family or group of friends who graduated from college, ask them to tell you how that decision has affected their life. Ask them what tips they have for how to be successful in school.

Parents and Kids: The following quote from Marianne Williamson was used in the movie to communicate an important message to Akeelah about striving for success. (Incidentally, the movie mistakenly attributes the quote to Nelson Mandela.) Together, read the quote out loud. Then talk about what each sentence means. Write down three ways you can let your own light shine.

> Our deepest fear is not that we are inadequate, our deepest fear is that we are powerful beyond measure. We ask ourselves, who am I to be brilliant, gorgeous, talented, and fabulous? Actually, who are you not to be? Your playing small doesn't serve the world. We were born to make manifest the glory of God that is within us. And as we let our own light shine, we unconsciously give other people permission to do the same.
>
> —*Marianne Williamson*

Parents and Kids: Together, brainstorm a list called "5 Things I Need from My Parent to Help Me Be Successful in School." Post it on the refrigerator door and for the next week make an effort to accomplish everything on the list.

Parents: Visit the website of the National Middle School Association (www.nmsa.org), and read "The Family Connection" and "Month of the Young Adolescent" sections. Make a list of ideas you would like to try for supporting your preteen's school success.

Parents and Kids: Look in a dictionary and find seven interesting words you don't know. Write each word and its definition on an index card or sheet of paper. Each day for the next week, choose one card to be the family's "new word of the day." Practice using that word in sentences while you're eating or driving around.

Nine to Five: Work

Sample Questions Asked by Middle-School Kids

?

Mom, what did you want to be when you were grown up?

What should I be when I grow up?

Can we talk about college and my future career?

What are good jobs?

Would an electrician be a good job to go into?

What do you do with all of our money, really?

How much money do you make?

What do you do at your job?

If you could have a different career than you have now, what would it be?

What jobs did you have that you liked most in the past?

A Few Things for Parents to Know

Adults often like to ask kids, "What do *you* want to be when you grow up?" When thinking of an answer, young people today have more options to choose from than ever before. And the questions from middle schoolers indicate a strong interest in exploring those options. Kids are curious about the work world.

Many adults spend a large portion of time working outside the home to earn a living. You may drop your child at school or hurry him out to the bus, spend eight to ten hours away from home, and then reappear at the end of the day to resume family life. Or you may have a job that requires you to travel for several days or weeks at a time or to work evenings and weekends. Sometimes children don't have a chance to see where their parents work and don't understand the jobs their parents have or how they settled on their type of employment.

As a middler who is beginning to think about the future, your young person could be confused about how her efforts in school might translate into a job someday. She may be wondering about the amazing variety of jobs available and how much she can expect to earn doing one thing or another. Some schools organize career days in which community members visit classrooms to discuss their occupations. The Ms. Foundation for Women promotes an event every year on the fourth Thursday in April called "Take Our Daughters and Sons to Work" to provide education and awareness about balancing work and family for both girls and boys. This chapter is offered in the same spirit—to deepen your child's understanding of the work you do and the workaday world in general.

Adulthood and employment go hand in hand in our society. Earning money sufficient to pay for life's necessities is a fundamental aspect of our culture and a major goal for young people seeking independence. In preparation for watching this movie with your middler, you might want to consider your personal values associated with work and money. For example, in what ways is your job meaningful to you? Would you say the work itself or the salary you earn is your primary motivator? What is your definition of a "good job"? For example, is it the satisfaction of helping others, or the thrill of being recognized as an expert in your field? Do you enjoy the challenge of constantly learning something new, or do you prefer steady and predictable tasks? Is it more important to you to have work that allows you freedom to do other things, or is the work you do a central part of your identity? What activities do you value more than your job? Do you think you have a good balance between your work life and family life? What aspects of employment or family life make it difficult to balance the two? Do you think the overall message about employment that you convey to your preteen is primarily positive or negative? What message would you like to convey?

Over the last thirty years there has been a major demographic shift in which more women are working outside the home. It has become commonplace for a woman to consider herself an equal wage earner with her partner. More women are preparing for careers, even as they also expect to raise children. A small but growing number of men are opting to be "stay-at-home dads," while their wives or partners are the principal providers of income for the family. These shifts in how we view the roles of men and women as workers will probably continue and are apt to affect your young person by opening up a broader range of choices.

Another significant change has been that women can more easily be hired in jobs that were traditionally held by men, and vice versa. For example, more women than ever before are entering fields involving math, science, and business; men are slightly more likely than in the past to be found in "helping professions," such as nursing and teaching. It is not unusual to see women working on road crews or as firefighters, and there has been a significant increase of women in military combat. How did your gender influence the type of work you chose to do? Do you perform a traditionally male or female job? If you work at something that has traditionally been occupied by the opposite sex, how has that been for you?

This chapter provides an opportunity for you to explore with your child differences among jobs in terms of salary and status. In the

United States people who work in entertainment, sports, and business are much better paid and enjoy a higher status than those who work in the nonprofit sector or those involved in the care and teaching of children. How does that reality reflect your own values? While many people in the U.S. avoid talk of social class, those making their living doing manual labor are often less respected than those working in offices and doing "mental" labor. What is your class background, and how has that influenced your choice of work? Would you be happy if your child chose to enter a traditionally working-class profession (factory worker, plumber, car repair person, construction worker, office worker), or will you encourage a more middle-class profession (administrator, doctor, lawyer, accountant, teacher)?

You might want to discuss with your child the training and/or education needed to pursue different types of employment. If he is interested in working while a teenager, he will probably be able to find an entry-level job in food service or retail that doesn't require any specialized education or training. A two-year or four-year college degree is required or preferred for numerous jobs, although it is no guarantee of employment. There are many young people with college degrees working in jobs different from their field of study. Advanced college degrees are required for some jobs, such as university-level teaching, counseling, medicine, and law. Teaching in public schools usually requires a four-year bachelor of arts degree plus a teaching credential specific to the state in which you reside. Jobs in the police department, fire department, and military involve their own specialized training and also might require education beyond high school. Government positions have a highly structured pay scale and often entail passing a civil service test. People who work in the arts as writers, artists, musicians, or dancers often persist with a talent and sometimes pursue specialized schooling to become recognized in their art. As your middler expresses interest in various possible occupational paths, it will be helpful to use resources such as the public library, a school guidance counselor, professional association websites, and adults who are employed in various jobs of interest to learn about the prerequisite training and education.

Just as different occupations require different levels of experience, training, or education, so, too, do they provide different levels of compensation. Job salaries sometimes depend on the amount of schooling or training a person has. For many entry-level jobs, particularly those requiring no more than a high-school diploma, the starting pay is often minimum wage. You can explain to your young person that minimum wage is the money per hour determined by the state in which you live as being the lowest amount an employer is permitted to pay workers. Generally, work that requires particular skills or education is better paid. Over the course of a lifetime, the more years of education an individual achieves, the higher the earning potential. In some instances, salary depends on developing a particular talent. Sports and entertainment figures, for example, usually start out with a talent that they pursue over time, and some are highly compensated for what they do. Office work may be better compensated than unskilled manual labor. Skilled manual laborers, such as electricians, plumbers, and construction workers, can be well paid but usually require extensive training or apprenticeships.

When we ask the age-old question "What do *you* want to be when you grow up?" we seem to imply that people choose one career path and stick with it for the rest of their lives. In reality, it is common to do more than one job or to have more than one career in a lifetime, especially as people are living longer. That question also suggests that young people are expected to know what kind of work they want to do as adults. The fact is that some individuals make a beeline towards a career starting at a young age, while many others take a more meandering path towards the work they do. Were you a "beeliner" or a "meanderer" in terms of finding your work or career? What factors do you think contributed to that? For example, was your employment pathway most influenced by your personality, upbringing, social class, the particular area in which you grew up, or the attitudes and opinions of others? Some people are highly motivated to move beyond their families of origin in terms of education and employment, and some people are satisfied to emulate their parents' choices. Which is more descriptive of you? As with all the topics in this book, your experiences, understanding, and values around work and money provide fertile ground on which to deepen your relationship with your middler.

On With The Show!

Movie:	**October Sky**
Year	1999
Length:	1 hour 48 minutes
MPAA rating:	PG
Key actors:	Jake Gyllenhaal as Homer Hickam
	Chris Cooper as John Hickam
	Laura Dern as Miss Riley
Director:	Joe Johnson

Movie Synopsis

October Sky is based on the book *Rocket Boys: A Memoir,* written by Homer Hickam. It tells the true story of Homer and three friends, who live in a small, mining town in West Virginia called Coalwood, and their passion to build rockets. The inspiration for this passion is Sputnik, the very first human attempt to put an object into space. The Russians launch Sputnik on October 4, 1957, when the four are in high school. The boys try again and again to design and launch the perfect rocket, learning from their mistakes as they go. A special teacher, Miss Riley, inspires them to pursue their dreams, and several townspeople provide material assistance. However, Homer's father, the mine supervisor, does little to encourage his son's interests. He wants Homer to follow in his footsteps and be a coalminer; he believes rocket scientists will be forced to find "real jobs" when public excitement about Sputnik dies down. Several events occur to weaken the boys' resolve to enter their work in a science fair competition. Homer's arguments with his father subside and then escalate again as he asserts his independence and desire for a life different from the one in which he was raised.

Cautions

The movie has minimal swearing *(son of a bitch, damn, hell)*. There is some slight sexual content and innuendo. For example, in one scene Homer receives advice from a friend about how to get his hands on a girl while watching a scary movie. In another, Homer's brother calls him and his friends "little sisters," reflecting the sexism of the time. No nudity is shown. Violence and alcohol abuse are minimal: Homer's father intervenes when a drunken man is physically abusing his stepson; this same man drives by Homer's house and shoots a bullet through a window, but no one is hurt. In another scene, the four boys are briefly shown to be slightly tipsy after visiting a neighbor to get 100-percent alcohol for their rocket fuel. No tobacco use is shown. Homer and his father exchange angry words about Homer's choices for his life. A man who helps Homer and his friends with their rockets dies in a mining accident, and his body is briefly shown, but there is no blood.

Movie Talking Points for Parents

★ Homer Hickam is fascinated by the launch of the Russian Sputnik and develops a passion for building rockets while he is still in high school. Later, he works as an engineer and trainer of astronauts for

NASA. How did you decide to pursue the work you do now? When did your interest in that work develop? What special training or education did it require? Have you always done one type of work, or have you had a variety of occupations? What do you most enjoy about the work you do now? What do you least enjoy about it? Do you ever think about doing something different? If so, what would you most like to do?

★ Homer announces at the family dinner table that he is going to build a rocket. His father says nothing, his brother laughs, and his mother says, "Well, just don't blow yourself up." When you were younger, what were your dreams or special interests? If you shared these with your parents, how did they react? If you didn't share them, what stopped you? Did your dreams or interests as a young person ever lead to work for which you were paid? How was your parents' support helpful to you when you were deciding what kind of work to pursue? If they weren't supportive, how would your life have been different if they had been?

★ Homer's family is typical of many during the 1950s in that his dad does paid work and his mother works at home, caring for the needs of her family. In your family of origin, did both your parents do paid work? If so, what jobs did they do? Did they work during the day or have different shifts? Were they paid by the hour, or were they salaried? If they worked before you started elementary school, who took care of you? How did your parents handle the balance between their work and family life? How does this compare to how you handle that balance now?

★ Homer and his friends are supported and encouraged by their teacher, Miss Riley, and Homer is enthralled with the famous rocket scientist, Wernher von Braun. Who supported you in pursuing the work you do? Were there any heroes in your life whom you wanted to emulate?

* The Rocket Boys are extremely persistent and overcome many obstacles to fulfill their dream of launching a successful rocket. Where in your life have you shown persistence in reaching a goal involving your work life, and what motivated you to keep going? What character attributes do you consider the most important as a working person?

* Homer's father (and Homer himself, for a brief time) does the highly dangerous work of a coalminer. What kind of work did your father and/or mother do? Was it dangerous? Is the work you do dangerous? What special skills or talents does your work require? Would you say you need more brains, brawn, or a balance of both for the work you do?

* Homer lives in a coalmining town in West Virginia but dreams of going away to college and working on rockets at Cape Canaveral. Did you want to live somewhere different from where you were raised? What do you think sparked this desire for a life different from your parents' and at what age did it emerge? How far— emotionally, physically, or both—have you journeyed from the place you were born or from the work your mom or your dad did?

* In *October Sky*, the coalminers decide to go on strike. Have you ever been a member of a labor union? Have you ever been involved in a strike? What can you tell your child about unions?

* Even though Homer is not strong in mathematical skills, his passion for rocketry carries him through many obstacles towards his goal of winning the science fair. What talents have you already noticed in your middle schooler that could translate into work in his or her future?

For Kids: What Do You Think?

October Sky tells the true story of Homer Hickam and his three friends, who are inspired to build rockets. When he is older, Homer becomes an engineer and works for NASA, so his early interest in rocket science led him to one of his careers (he is now a full-time writer). What do you wonder about the world of working adults? Now is the time to ask any questions you have.

To get your creative juices flowing, share your answers to the following questions with your parent or parents and see what they say!

★ Homer's father is the mine supervisor, and he wants Homer to follow in his footsteps. Do you think your mom or dad would like you to do the same work they do? Do you have any interest in doing what they do? What kind of work do you think you would like to do when you're older? What is it about that work that is attractive to you?

★ Miss Riley tells Homer, "Math is not one of your favorite subjects. You can't dream your way out of Coalwood." She meant that he would have to learn math in order to be a rocket scientist. What would you have to learn to do the work you'd like to do as an adult?

★ For Homer, the work his father does is easy to understand: he is in charge of supervising men who work in a coal mine. Your mom or your dad might do work that is harder to understand. What questions do you have about what your parents do for a living? What do you think led your parents to choose the kind of work they do? Do you think they enjoy or do not enjoy the work they do? How can you tell?

★ Wernher von Braun, a famous rocket scientist who was instrumental in the early days of space exploration, inspires Homer. Who do you know or know about who inspires you? What adults in your life encourage you?

★ The Rocket Boys are so excited about building rockets it is easy to imagine them spending all their time doing so. What, if anything, would you spend 100 percent of your time doing if you could?

★ Homer and his friends enjoy building and launching rockets so much that they walk eight miles to their launching site. They also rip up heavy railroad ties to sell in order to have money to purchase the kind of steel they need. What activities have you done alone or with friends that you enjoyed so much you were willing to work really hard to do them? What made these activities interesting? Are any of these activities things adults do for work?

★ A miner who helps Homer with his rockets is killed in a mining accident, and Homer's dad is injured in another. What worries, if any, do you have about your mom or dad and the work they do?

★ When Homer's father is injured in a mining accident, his mother says the mining company won't pay for all the hospital and medical bills. What issues about money come up in your household the most? What word would you use to describe each of your parents' attitudes about money: worried, comfortable, secretive, angry, relaxed. If none of these is a good fit, what word or phrase is? What, if anything, would you like to change about the way money affects your family?

✓ Your Turn

Now it's your turn to write down any questions you would like to ask one or both of your parents about work, careers, or earning money. What do you *really* want to know?

_____

_____

_____

_____

_____

_____

_____

_____

_____

_____

Activities

Kids: All jobs take at least some brains, but some jobs also involve more "hands-on" activities, so a combination of brains and muscles are required. Make a list of all the jobs you can think of that are mostly "thinking" jobs in one column, and jobs that involve both thinking and physical work in another column. Then get additional ideas from a parent or other adults to add more jobs to your list. Select five or six jobs that sound the most interesting to you personally.

Parents and Kids: After doing the above activity, go to www.salary.com and find out what people typically earn in the five or six jobs you selected from your list. What jobs are better paid? Which are less well paid? Then go to www.occupationalinfo.org and look up a description of each job. Which sounds like a job you would like to have?

Kids: Ask your parent to help you find someone in your community who does the job from the above activities that sounds the most interesting to you. See if your parent can make arrangements for you to spend an hour watching (or shadowing) that person doing their job.

Parents and Kids: Parents, make a list of all the regular expenses that you pay every month, such as a mortgage or rent, utilities, food, clothing, car or other transportation, childcare, entertainment, and so on. Ask your child to guess how much you spend in each category and then write down approximately what you really spend.

Kids: Go to http://history.nasa.gov/sputnik/ and read about how the Russian launch of Sputnik in 1957 changed the world. Ask a grandparent or someone else you know who was at least a teenager in 1957 what they remember about the event.

Parents: Make a list of every job you have ever had for which you earned money, starting with selling lemonade, lawn mowing, or babysitting, for instance. Next to each job put how much you were paid. Share this with your middler, and also discuss your current salary and how it has changed over time.

Parents: Go to www.daughtersandsonstowork.org/ and read about how to organize a "Bring Your Son or Daughter to Work Day" at your place of employment. Consider spearheading the effort to do it!

Looking to the Future: Adulthood

Sample Questions Asked by Middle-School Kids

What does it feel like to be a grown-up?

Were you scared about growing up when you were a kid?

What were your dreams when you were little?

Would you stand by the decisions I make in life?

Is it fun to be an adult?

Is it hard being an adult?

What is it like to be a parent?

When we grow up, how hard is it in life to keep up on the bills?

Do you get more respect when you are older?

Where do you want me to be living in 10 years?

⭐ A Few Things for Parents to Know

Early adolescence is accompanied by cognitive abilities and societal messages that lead kids to begin thinking about their future. Questions from the research remind us that as early as middle school, young people may be thinking about what it will be like to become an adult. While leaving home and taking responsibility for oneself are still in the distant future, this is an important area of discussion for parents and preteens because it can be a topic that evokes anxiety on the part of both. While parents may view the launching of children as the culmination of years of childrearing, they also may worry about whether they have fully prepared their young people for successful adulthood. And while kids may view leaving home as the long-awaited mark of adult independence, they also may be frightened by the magnitude of what it means to be fully self-sufficient.

While issues of maturity and particular domains of privilege and responsibility are touched on in several other chapters in this book (Chapters 6, 8, and 10), this chapter is focused on your child's process towards achieving a sense of personal identity and self-reliance and on your involvement in helping or hindering that process. The movie we have selected, *Real Women Have Curves*, portrays a father who has accepted his daughter's decision about her own life and a mother who has difficulty doing so. The main character, despite her own ambivalence and fear, finds the inner strength to take responsibility for her own decisions and to move towards the life she wants.

If you're like most parents, you probably view adolescence as a time of preparing for adulthood. Families, schools, and communities all share in the job of teaching young people about adult roles and responsibilities. As our culture becomes increasingly complex, so do the tasks and skills needed by a young person to take responsibility for his own life and livelihood. In addition, the definition of adulthood can be confusing for parents and adolescents because on both sides there is often a great deal of emotion involved in letting go. Legally, an adult is someone who has reached the age of majority, which is 18 years of age in the United States. While some parents are ready to relinquish authority over their child at age 18, many consider their child's level of maturity to be a more definitive guideline for determining adulthood. Due to the high cost of living, some parents continue to assume financial responsibility for their child, helping him to attend college or a trade school, or offering other support until he can establish himself independently. Today in the U.S., nearly half of 18- to 24-year-olds live with their parents.

Expectations about when and how a young person will leave home to begin an independent life vary from one family to another. Even within the same family, different people may have different notions about the "right" age for children to move out of the home and the "best" choices for plans post–high school. Perhaps you and your child's other parent have different preferences based on your own personal experiences in leaving your parents' home. Did you leave home the summer after high-school graduation to attend college somewhere, or did you continue to live at home and commute to college? Did you go to work full-time at age 18 and rent your own apartment, or did you stay with Mom and Dad until you got married? What do you envision for your own child? Do you have hopes that she will follow in your footsteps, or do you hope she will find a different path? Can you envision her living a thousand miles away from you, or do you expect her to settle in her hometown? Do you want her to follow her own dreams, or do you hope she will compromise for the sake of family solidarity? Now, while your child is still in middle school, is a good time to begin the conversation about such matters.

Part of your discussion might focus on providing a realistic understanding of what you as an adult are responsible for and what steps you took to begin handling all the tasks you have. While it's obvious to you what you do, your child only sees a part of the many tasks and responsibilities you handle on a daily basis: fulfilling your work commitments, caring for your family, organizing schedules, maintaining your home, shopping for groceries, cooking meals, paying bills, participating in your community, socializing with friends and family . . . the list is long for most parents. Furthermore, you've probably always done these things within his lifetime so he doesn't know how you learned them. He doesn't know much about preparing to be a working adult or making important decisions like becoming a parent. You might also use this time to reflect on your own feelings about being an adult. What is fun about it? What is challenging? How did you get to where you are? Reassure your preteen that adulthood happens in stages and that you will be there to help him make the transition.

Milestones on the road to adulthood vary greatly based on ethnic background, religious affiliation, and social class. For example, Jewish parents sometimes arrange bar mitzvahs (for sons) or bat mitzvahs (for daughters) at age 13, signifying they are ready to assume responsibility for their own spiritual life. Mexican families in the Catholic tradition sometimes provide an elaborate "coming of age" ritual called the *quinceañera* for daughters at age 15, which affirms her connection to the church and her entry into adulthood. The sunrise ceremony or *na'ii'ees*, traditionally a four-day event, is performed when an Apache girl reaches puberty. These rituals help young people make the transition to adulthood more gracefully. Unfortunately, appropriate rituals are lacking for most adolescents.

Some secular milestones have evolved that are more widespread. For example, passing the test for a driver's license is commonly accepted by both parents and adolescents as an important step toward adulthood, a signal of more freedom for the adolescent and greater trust by the parent. Graduating from high school, joining the military, or graduating from college are other examples of common milestones that attest to a young person's ability to stay on task and to set and accomplish goals. What markers will be important to you as you watch your child gain in maturity and approach the end of adolescence? What family or religious rituals are you planning that will help your child transition to independence? How do you imagine your relationship with your child will change as adulthood approaches?

Establishing an independent identity is one of the key tasks of a young adult. As an adolescent forms a sense of who she is, she may begin to articulate the ways she is similar to and different from her parents. This process is difficult for biological children but especially problematic for a child raised by adoptive parents. Questions about why she was relinquished for adoption and whom she resembles may prompt a desire to initiate the process of reconnecting with her birth parents. Adoptive parents may be afraid of being replaced in their child's affections by a birth mother or father. But, just as a parent can love multiple children, so can children love multiple parents. Supporting and encouraging her efforts to reconnect to her roots can, in fact, bring you closer.

The prospect of sons and daughters growing up and leaving home brings mixed emotions for most parents as well as for the young people themselves. There is both joy and sorrow to be found in launching children into their adult lives. Talking about it now, while your child is still in middle school, can help both of you look forward to the future with positive expectations.

On With The Show!

Movie:	**Real Women Have Curves**
Year:	2002
Length:	1 hour 26 minutes
MPAA rating:	PG-13
Key actors:	America Ferrera as Ana Garcia
	Lupe Ontiveros as Carmen Garcia
	Ingrid Oliu as Estela Garcia
	Felipe DeAlba as the grandfather
Director:	Patricia Cardoso

Movie Synopsis

Real Women Have Curves tells the story of contemporary 18-year-old Ana Garcia, a Mexican-American girl from a working class family. The family lives in East Los Angeles, but Ana takes two buses every day to attend Beverly Hills High School. A teacher there encourages her to apply for college, but Ana resists. On the last day of school, Ana triumphantly quits her waitress job, only to encounter her mother's wrath when she returns home. Her mother expects her to work as she herself has done since age 13. Ana's sister, Estela, owns a small garment factory, and her mother insists that Ana work there just as her mother does. The factory employs a handful of women who hand-sew gowns that are sold for $600 at Bloomingdale's, while Estela's company is paid only $18 for each dress. Ana is full of angst about this injustice and hates the factory, even as she dutifully acquiesces to her mother's wishes that she work there. Meanwhile, Ana has her first love affair, with an Anglo boy; finally finishes her college application; and continues to struggle with her mother as she makes her way from dependent child to self-determined adult.

 ## Cautions

Real Women Have Curves has minimal swearing, but at one point Ana says, "Fuck you" to her mother in response to her mother's criticism. Ana engages in a relationship with a boy her age from her high school. He is going off to college, and she conscientiously plans for their first sexual intercourse by buying condoms. The sex scene is sensitively and tastefully done, portraying a respectful and mutually chosen encounter with love and lightness. There is no full nudity. Ana is a voluptuous young woman, and her weight is an issue with her mother, who often says shaming things to her. Ana is much more accepting of her own body, and that attitude is affirmed by her young lover. In one scene of the movie Ana and the other women who work in her sister's factory are all miserable in the heat, and Ana encourages them to strip down to their bras and panties. All but her mother comply as they compare their "imperfect" bodies and laugh and dance with each other.

Movie Talking Points for Parents

★ In *Real Women Have Curves,* Ana has just graduated from high school and has quit her job at a restaurant, but she is pressured by her mother into working in her sister's dress factory. What messages about family solidarity were you given when you were a teenager? Did you feel your family needed you and counted on your help, or were you free to pursue your own dreams?

★ Ana comes from a working class family of Mexican-Americans, while her boyfriend, Jimmy, is from an upper-middle-class, white family that can afford trips to Europe. The two of them have different expectations for their plans after high school. How did your family's class background or ethnic background influence your options and choices as you finished high school and moved into adulthood?

★ At the end of the movie, Ana is shown living in New York City, completely on her own and happy to face her new life. Was your transition to your independence gradual or abrupt? What were the major milestones of that transition? Did you have to "take a stand" for what you wanted to do with your life, or did you agree with what your parents wanted for you? Do you think you will repeat your parents' methods or do things differently?

★ In the movie Ana's father is reluctant to loan Estela money to pay her rent because he wants to see her make her own way. Later, it is unclear what financial support Ana gets from her parents to pursue her dream to attend Columbia University in New York City. Did your parents help you financially after you left high school? How was their financial support (or lack of financial support) helpful or unhelpful to you in becoming an adult? What financial support do you expect to provide for your child after age 18?

★ Ana's mother asserts that she can teach Ana everything she needs to know: how to sew, cook, and take care of her husband. What skills did your mother or father think were important for you to know by the time you were age 18? What methods did they use to teach you? Was there any life skill that you found out you lacked when you left home? What life skills do you think are important to impart to your child (for example, cooking, doing laundry, cleaning house, balancing a checkbook, handling money, sticking to a goal)? What do you do to help your child learn the life skills you think are most important?

★ Even though Ana has graduated from high school, her mother still wants to dictate what Ana does with her time and expects Ana to put the needs of her family first. She has difficulty with the idea of letting Ana separate from her and from the family, and she does things to try to prevent Ana from leaving. What was your experience in leaving home as a young adult? Was there a great deal of struggle with your mom or dad when you made the transition to adulthood, or was it smooth? What issues of your growing maturity and self-determination caused friction? How were they resolved? As you think about the future when your middler will finish high school and leave home, how do you feel? What do you anticipate will be difficult about that?

★ In many ways Ana is a mature and responsible young woman. She attends Beverly Hills High School despite living far away in East Los Angeles. Her grades are good enough to be accepted at Columbia University. She buys a condom and hands it to her partner before having sex for the first time. She chooses to go to college in New York City and heads off on her own to do so, even without her mother's blessing. In what ways did your maturity match Ana's when you were 18? In what ways were you lacking in maturity? What behaviors in your child will signal to you that she or he is developing maturity?

WHAT KIDS *REALLY* WANT TO ASK

★ Ana experiences some anger and confusion as she wrestles with decisions about what to do with her life, and feels the competing pull of her own heart versus her family's wishes. In what ways did you feel confused or unsure during your transition to adulthood? What things did you worry about?

★ Ana's mother appears to be unhappy with her lot in life and behaves in ways that are emotionally manipulative. She sulks in her room so that Ana will stay home from school; she imagines she is pregnant instead of acknowledging menopause; she refuses to give Ana her blessing to go to college. In what ways did your mom or dad have difficulty in helping you enter adulthood?

★ One interpretation of Ana's behavior in the movie is that she is conflicted between what she can envision for her future and what her parents expect for her. What expectations do you have for your son or daughter? Do you have different expectations based on gender? (For example, do you think a career is less important for a daughter than a son?) How would you feel if your child chose a path different from the one you think is best?

For Kids: What Do You Think?

Real Women Have Curves is about 18-year-old Ana Garcia, who is making the transition from high school to her adult life. Her mother wants her to go to work to help the family, but Ana is torn. She wants to go to college. You may have questions about being an adult. The truth is that opinions vary about when a person becomes an adult. It can have a lot to do with the culture you live in and the expectations of your parents. Watching this movie with a parent will give you the opportunity to think about and discuss adulthood.

Here are some questions to get a conversation started.

★ Ana loves her family but wants to do more with her life than stay in her hometown and work in her sister's factory. How do you feel about the life your family has in your hometown? Do you see yourself staying there as an adult? How would you feel about living in a state or country different from where your parents live when you are an adult?

★ Ana finds in her grandfather the emotional support and encouragement her parents are unable to offer. For example, she enlists the help of her grandfather to go on a date with her boyfriend. And her grandfather encourages Ana to forge her own path when he tells her, "You are my gold. Now I want you to find yours." How do you feel about the amount of support and encouragement your parents give you for your future goals? What relative or adult friend in your life can you ask to help you when you feel you can't ask a parent?

★ Ana's teacher encourages her to apply to college, but her parents want her to stay and help the family. In the end, she decides to go. What are your parents' expectations about you going to college? In what ways do you think college would be a good idea for you? In what ways are you not sure? In what ways would going to college help you become an adult?

★ Ana acts in some ways that are really mature and a few ways that aren't so mature. What are some mature things Ana did in the movie that you think are important for being seen as an adult?

★ At the end of the movie, Ana is in New York City, ready to start her adult life. What knowledge and skills do you think you need to learn in order to be ready to be on your own? What do your parents think are the most important life skills for you to learn in order to be on your own? How do you think you will learn those things?

★ Ana is in a relationship with a boy who asks if she is going to Europe for the summer and who says, "Things are too easy in the U.S." But Ana's mother and sister work in a factory and her father works as a gardener. In what ways are you more privileged than kids you go to school with? In what ways are you less privileged? How do you think becoming an adult will be easier or more difficult for you than for other kids you go to school with?

★ Ana's mother started working when she was just 13 years old, so she expects Ana to go to work and get married as well. In some ways she seems to be jealous of Ana and wishes she could be young again and have the freedom to go off to college. In what ways do you think your future as an adult will be different from your parents' adult lives? In what ways do you think your parents wish they could do things over?

★ When Ana graduated from high school, she had dreams of going to college in New York City. What are your dreams for after high school? What might you want to do when you are an adult?

✓ Your Turn

Now it's your turn to write down any questions you would like to ask your dad or mom about being an adult. What do you *really* want to know?

_____

_____

_____

_____

_____

_____

💡 Activities

Parents and Kids: Do the following as a joint research project with the parent interviewing students and with the child interviewing adults. (This could be an interesting school project.)

* Interview 20 adults and ask each of them what their opinion is about when one becomes an adult, using these options: graduation from high school, age 18, graduation from college, full-time employment, living on one's own, getting married, having children, or other (they can choose).

* Interview 20 middle-school students and ask the same questions.

* Compare the answers.

Parents: Write a letter to your child telling all of the things you wish for him in his adult years and give any advice you think would be helpful as he embarks on his adult life. Save the letter and present it to your child on his eighteenth birthday.

Kids: Research the legal age in your state for the following:

* Marriage   * Drinking alcohol

* Driving a car   * Owning a firearm

Then have a dinner table discussion about these ages. Do you think it's fair, or unfair? When do you think you'll be ready for these things? What are your parents' opinions about when you'll be ready? How will you prepare for these privileges?

Parents and Kids: Separately, each of you make a "Checklist for Adulthood." List all the things you think people need to know before living on their own. Compare your lists. Then make a plan for who will teach these things to the kids in your family. Keep this checklist, and every year on the kids' birthdays, pull it out and check off all the things that were learned in the past year.

Parents and Kids: Discuss the events that seem most like steps towards adulthood for a young person, for example, graduation from middle school, getting a driver's license, graduation from high school, first paycheck. Which of these would you like to mark with a celebration or ritual? What kind of celebration would it be?

Is This Just the Way It Is?
Life

> ### Sample Questions Asked by Middle-School Kids
>
> Why is there so much killing in the world?
>
> What is the point of living?
>
> Why are we on Earth?
>
> Why do people have to die?
>
> Are people usually nicer than they seem?
>
> Why do people love each other?
>
> Why do some people have complications and others don't?
>
> Why do so many people have no respect at all, and why are people so mean to others?
>
> Why do people have bad tempers?
>
> Why do people do drugs?

⭐ A Few Things for Parents to Know

Of the twelve chapters in *What Kids REALLY Want to Ask*, this may be one of the most challenging for both you and your child. The movie we have selected, *Pay It Forward*, conveys powerful images and messages pertaining to loving, caring, and sharing. It also starkly addresses some of the darker realities of life like homelessness, drug and alcohol addiction, disrupted family relations, social cruelty, violence, and death. We hope this chapter will help you address some of these issues with your children.

As young people approach the early years of adolescence, they begin to acquire the ability to think beyond themselves and to have a greater awareness of the larger world. They start to contemplate abstract concepts that were not in their realm of thought when they were younger. The questions posed by the kids in the research reflect this tendency to think more about the "bigger picture."

Adults also ponder these complex questions, wondering why people have to die, the reasons behind human acts of cruelty, why so many are homeless or addicted to drugs and alcohol. We struggle with how to respond when these issues touch our personal lives. We may wish our children wouldn't ask these big questions, especially when we haven't come to any clear conclusions ourselves. Often we would like to shelter them from the harsh truths of life's adversities. But odds are your preteen *is* wondering about some of these topics, so even if you don't have all the answers, it's important to create an opportunity to discuss them. The following background information may be helpful as you enter into conversation with your middler.

Perhaps you have heard it said that most Americans are just a few paychecks or one natural disaster away from being homeless. In 2005, Hurricane Katrina illustrated the truth of that statement, when hundreds of thousands lost their homes and were forced to seek temporary shelter and to survive under horrible conditions. Large-scale catastrophes aside, every year in the U.S. close to three million people (including one million children) are homeless, a number that has been steadily increasing since 1990. Families are the fastest growing segment of the homeless population. In the majority of cases, homelessness is temporary, until housing assistance from social agencies or family members is obtained, but about one fourth of these families have been homeless for at least five years. The movie for this chapter depicts the struggles of the chronically homeless. These individuals are most likely to live in cities, and you may have observed their plight firsthand.

Homelessness and poverty are related, and both are extremely complex social problems. As reflected in the questions from the research, your young adolescent may wonder why some people experience such hardships in their lives and others don't. To promote empathy and understanding, you may want to convey to your young person that the homeless are not bad people, but rather well-meaning individuals who are victims of adverse life circumstances. Many have limited education and job skills, and at least half struggle with alcohol and drug addiction and/or a major mental illness that impedes their ability to earn a living wage.

The topic of alcohol and drug abuse is another example of one of the darker realities of life about which preteens have questions. While Chapter 3, "Parents Are People, Too," offers the chance to talk about your perspective on the casual use of alcohol and drugs, this chapter raises the issue of addiction. Once again, to convey an attitude of empathy, it may be helpful to explain that addiction can be best understood as a brain disease, not a personality flaw. Most addicts started out as casual users, sometimes in response to social pressure and sometimes as an attempt to cope with life-stress and unhappiness. Unfortunately, their brains were hijacked by the chemicals in the alcohol and drugs, leading to a physical addiction. Breaking the addiction usually requires incredible personal determination and often professional assistance as well. You may also want to let your middler know that recent research shows that the adolescent brain is especially susceptible to the addictive effects of alcohol and drugs.

While most of us probably believe that human beings are inherently good and kind, the sad reality is that some people behave in ways that are hurtful and mean. It is likely that your preteen has witnessed, either firsthand or in the media, instances of social cruelty. Within the home, this can take the form of domestic violence against children or adult partners. Within the school and community, this can take the form of bullying and fighting, and the cruelty can escalate to involve the use of weapons in any of those environments. If you have personal experience as a victim, you'll need to decide how much you want your middler to know about what happened. It's a good idea to let her know that being mistreated is not the victim's fault and that asking for help is not a sign of weakness. She also needs to hear the message that no human being deserves to be treated unkindly. Make it clear that it is an act of love and respect for herself to walk away from any situation in which she feels at risk of physical or emotional harm and that she can count on your support if she ever has to do so.

Explaining to your young person the origins of social cruelty and violence, and why some people are mean to each other, again means acknowledging a complicated issue with no simple answer. People who behave that way are usually dealing with deep-seated feelings of unhappiness and anger, which often stem from negative childhood experiences. The absence of impulse control may also be a contributing factor.

Perhaps the biggest existential question, and the one with the fewest satisfactory answers, is why people have to die. The very fact that this question was posed by kids in the research tells us that preteens have an understanding of the finality of death and realize that death can happen to them and to people they know. Talking openly about the emotions associated with death will help your young person accept his feelings as normal and acceptable. Let him know that it's okay to feel afraid or sad or angry about the fact that people die. It's also important to acknowledge that everyone grieves differently and at their own pace, so there is no right or wrong way to feel when someone dies. If you haven't done so already, this may also be a good time to share any religious or spiritual beliefs that help you make sense of the cycle of life and death. Opportunities to discuss the topic of death also arise in Chapter 1 and in Chapter 8.

As your young person begins to wrestle with matters of human existence and hardship, you may wonder what to offer by way of answers. Don't be afraid to say, "I wish I knew the answer to your question, but I don't." The fact is there are no simple explanations. But engaging her in the dialogue, asking her what she thinks, sharing your own perspectives, and even admitting your own uncertainties will convey to her that these are indeed questions worth considering. Puzzling through dilemmas of the human experience may help her, as well as you, clarify personal and family values in these matters.

On With The Show!

Movie:	**Pay It Forward**
Year:	2000
Length:	2 hours 3 minutes
MPAA rating:	PG-13
Key actors:	Haley Joel Osment as Trevor McKinney
	Helen Hunt as Arlene McKinney
	Kevin Spacey as Eugene Simonet
Director:	Mimi Leder

Movie Synopsis

Pay It Forward tells the story of seventh grader Trevor McKinney, who is challenged by his social studies teacher, Eugene Simonet, to "think of an idea that will change the world and put it into action." Trevor, possessing wisdom well beyond his 11 years, comes up with a plan to do a good deed for three people that they are unable to do for themselves. The only stipulation is that each of them must in turn help three other people, or "pay it forward." As he enacts his plan, Trevor reaches out to several less fortunate individuals, including a homeless drug addict; his own hard-working, blue-collar, single-parent mother; and a classmate tormented by peers. The movie depicts ways in which these people are touched by Trevor. By the end of the movie, Trevor has directly or indirectly changed many lives for the better and has earned the respect and admiration of family, friends, and strangers for his love, altruism, and optimism. Sadly, his own life is tragically cut short, but his inspiration lives on in those who knew him.

Cautions

The movie exposes viewers to the harsh realities of homelessness, drug and alcohol addiction, domestic conflict, peer-group bullying, and untimely death. The opening scene depicts a robbery/hostage situation, and although guns are shown, no shots are fired. Later in the film gun shots are fired in a hospital waiting room, but the target is the floor, not humans. There are several scenes portraying homeless individuals living in alleys and junkyards and scrounging for food and warmth. There are a dozen or so instances of swearing throughout the film, including the terms *bullshit, ass, asshole, rat bastard, dick head,* and *son of a bitch.* Trevor's mother is an alcoholic who is struggling to overcome her addiction. In several scenes she is shown drinking liquor and smoking marijuana, and at one point she refers to herself as a "drunk." In one scene she and Trevor argue about her drinking, and she slaps him across the face. This is followed by sincere remorse, an apology, and a pledge to change her ways, which she succeeds in doing. In one scene, Trevor's homeless friend is shown high on drugs in a seedy hotel room. There is one lovemaking scene between Arlene and Eugene. It is tender and sensitive, with dim lighting, and no nudity is shown. Eugene tells a story of horrible abuse he suffered as a child at the hands of his father, who doused him with gasoline and set him on fire. While viewers don't witness the abuse he describes, the scarring on Eugene's body is evident. At the end of the movie, Trevor is stabbed and killed by a classmate, while trying to save his friend Adam from getting beaten up.

Movie Talking Points for Parents

★ Arlene McKinney struggles with alcohol addiction but maintains a commitment to doing right by her son, Trevor. In order to do this, she must admit her weaknesses to Trevor. What limitations, if any, have you overcome for the sake of your children? What improvements would you like to make in yourself or the way you live your life?

★ When Mr. Simonet challenges the class to think of one action to change the world, Trevor asks him what *he* has ever done to change the world. What would you say in response to this question?

★ Trevor's mother is upset when she sees a homeless man in their house and tells Trevor, "You can't have a friend like that." Later, she threatens to shoot the man when she finds him in the garage. How do you feel about homeless people? Have you ever spoken to a homeless person or offered to help a homeless person? Why or why not? Would you encourage or discourage your middler from giving money to a homeless person on the street?

★ If you had the opportunity to "pay it forward" and do big favors for three people, what would you do and for whom?

★ Trevor routinely sees the good in and expects the best from other people. How easy or difficult is it for you to look beyond such things as appearance and get to know people before judging them? Can you think of a time when your first impression of someone was unfavorable but changed once you got to know him or her?

★ The homeless drug addict stops a woman from jumping off a bridge by pleading with her, "Do me a favor. Save my life." He realized that saving the woman's life would make his own life meaningful. What do you think gives life meaning? What accomplishments in your own life do you consider most meaningful?

★ When she gets upset, Arlene turns to alcohol to numb her feelings.

How do you deal with stress in your own life? Is this an area you need to improve on? What advice would you give your young person about how to handle stress?

★ Eugene tells Arlene the story of the horrid abuse his father inflicted on him when he was a boy. Then he tells Arlene that Trevor's father may end up hurting Trevor because "all he has to do is not love him." What do you think are some of the reasons abusive parents have trouble loving their children? In your experience of your own life or the lives of friends or family, what kinds of human damage result from childhood abuse and lack of parental love?

★ Near the end of the movie Arlene finds her estranged homeless mother and forgives her for the unpleasant childhood she had. Is there anyone in your life from whom you are estranged or whom you have trouble forgiving for things they did to you when you were young? What makes it difficult to let go of the past? How might your life be different if you were to forgive this person?

★ At the end of *Pay It Forward* Arlene suffers one of the most tragic of human experiences when her son is killed. What is the most heartbreaking death you have had to deal with? What can you tell your child about why death occurs and how people endure the death of a loved one?

For Kids: What Do You Think?

Pay It Forward tells the story of Trevor McKinney, who has difficulty accepting the misfortune around him and wants to make the world a better place. Are there things about life that you have trouble making sense of? Do you ever dream about how you would change the world?

To get your creative juices flowing for a great conversation, share your answers to the following questions with your parent or parents and see what they say!

★ *Pay It Forward* shows several huge acts of generosity, as when the wealthy attorney gives his expensive sports car to the reporter. What is the most generous thing you have ever done for someone? What generous things have been done for you? How did you feel when you were being generous to another person? How did you feel when someone was generous to you?

★ Trevor gets upset and frustrated after a fight with his mother and tries to run away from home. Have you ever been so upset you just wanted to run away from your problems rather than face them? How do you think this would make your problems better or worse?

★ Trevor tells Mr. Simonet the world expects nothing from seventh graders. What is your opinion about that? As you look into the future, what do you think the world expects from you?

★ As one of his first acts of generosity, Trevor invites a homeless man into his home and gives him food and a place to sleep. What do you think of this? Would it scare you to talk to a homeless person?

★ If you had the opportunity to "pay it forward" and do big favors for three people, what would you do and for whom?

★ Several of the characters in *Pay It Forward* are alcoholics, including Trevor's mother and grandmother. Is there someone close to you who drinks too much? How do you feel when you're around this person? What do you know about why people use alcohol and drugs?

★ Trevor starts his "pay it forward" plan because he wants to make the world a better place. In what ways is the world a disappointment to you? What would you do to change the world? How might one person make the world a better place?

★ Trevor steps into the middle of a bullying situation to help his friend Adam, and there are tragic consequences. Have you ever witnessed a classmate being bullied? How did you feel? What would you do to help someone who is being bullied? Who could you turn to for help with that?

★ Trevor died tragically and at too young an age, but he left a lasting impression on those who knew him. Have you ever lost a close friend or family member to death? In what ways does that person still live on in your memories or in the way you live your life?

✓ Your Turn

Now it's your turn to write down any questions you would like to ask one or both of your parents about the way life is and the nature of people. Be bold and ask away! Offer to take their answers in writing if it makes it easier for them.

_____

_____

_____

_____

_____

_____

Activities

Kids: Make the next week "Random Acts of Kindness Week." Each day, do one small act of kindness for someone without being asked to do it. For example, if you're standing in line, let the person behind you go in front of you; or if you see someone drop something, stop and pick it up for them. Keep a list of all the random acts of kindness you perform. Ask your family and friends to do the same and share your experiences with each other.

Parents: Find out where the nearest homeless shelter or soup kitchen is (look in the Yellow Pages under "social service organizations"). Call and schedule a time for you and your young person to go and volunteer for a few hours. Afterwards, talk about how it felt to be there and what you learned about yourself and the people being served.

Parents and Kids: Separately write a list of ten reasons not to drink alcohol or use drugs, and compare and discuss your lists. Then, write down ten ways to relax without using alcohol or drugs.

Kids: For your next birthday, ask family and friends to bring something to donate to a local children's services agency instead of giving you a present. Ask your parent to drive you to the agency to deliver the donations.

Parents and Kids: Talk about how you would want to be remembered or what you hope people would say about you if you died tomorrow. Then write a eulogy for yourself.

Parents and Kids: Play "find the silver lining in the gray cloud" around the dinner table. Each person names one thing that didn't go well that day. This is the gray cloud. For example, "On my way home from work, every traffic light was red" or "My pencil broke in math class, so I had to borrow one from the kid sitting next to me." Next, each person has to take a positive outlook and name one silver lining in the gray cloud. For example, "Every traffic light was red, so I had more time to listen to my music" or "I had to borrow a pencil, so I got to meet someone new."

Parents and Kids: The next time you're angry at someone and feel like yelling at them, try closing your eyes and counting to ten slowly. Then ask if you can hold their hand or give them a hug. Notice how this feels.

Acknowledgments

Joint Acknowledgments

First and foremost, we wish to thank the hundreds of anonymous middle-school students who responded to Rhonda's survey of what kids really want to ask their parents. The sincerity and importance of your questions was our guiding imperative for writing this book and we are honored to bring your thoughts to a wider audience.

Thanks to our publisher, Meredith Rutter, for sharing our vision and enthusiasm for this project, and giving us the chance to turn our dream into reality. Thanks also to editor Pat Moore and publicist Kate Bandos for applying their unique talents so ably for this book.

Rhonda's Acknowledgments

When I first met Margaret Pevec, she was a graduate student in my Parent-Child Relationships course and this book was a mere glimmer of an idea. Thus began a cooperative venture that has been one of the most significant experiences of my life. Thank you, Margaret, for joining me in friendship and in writing. With you I experienced an astonishing synergy of ideas and energy that enabled this book to happen, and I relish the thought of future collaborations.

Countless friends expressed interest and encouragement that provided momentum for this project. I especially wish to acknowledge Nancy Barbour and Kathleen Walker.

I have been blessed for half a century by the love of my mother, Elizabeth McGuire Bohn. This book is a testimony to her magnificence as a woman and role model of persistence, compassion, creativity, and intelligence.

I am grateful to my husband and partner in life, Brian Bialik, for sharing this journey with me. Your steadfast confidence and pride in my capabilities and your unconditional love sustained me through periods of doubt and bolstered my excitement in moments of accomplishment.

Finally, I offer heartfelt thanks to my daughters, Jenna Bialik and Logan Bialik, for allowing me to experience firsthand the joys of parenting children through the middle-school years. Together, the two of you fill my life with wonder, pride, and joy, and for that I dedicate this book to you both.

Margaret's Acknowledgments

Many years ago, when I was immersed in some of my most challenging years as a mother, I had a flash of intuition that I would find my voice as a writer in my 50s and beyond. Thanks to Rhonda Richardson, that intuition has been born into reality with this book. I extend to her my deep gratitude for inviting me to be her co-author. It has been an ongoing joy and delight to work with you and it will stand as my benchmark for successful collaboration. I hope this is only the first of many more fun and exciting creations for us!

My mother, Alma Dawson, and brother, Lawrence Pevec, have been enthusiastic supporters of whatever I do. It is with deepest appreciation that I acknowledge their sustaining presence in my life.

Throughout my adult life, special friends have been there for me in a variety of ways, especially in an exchange of ideas and experiences as parents or mentors of children. Chief among those with whom I am still in relationship are Illene Pevec, Halimah and Elia Van Tuyl, Oriana Mead, Murwani Adams-Combs, Deva Luna, Terra Lee, Emmah Smyth, Dawn Kimble, Dennise Brown, Monty Rowell, Elouise Joseph, and in memoriam to Laurel Dickerson. I bless the day I met each of you.

Appendix

450 Questions That Middle-School Students Want to Ask Their Parents

The following pages provide a list of questions posed by children ages 10 to 14 in answer to the following inquiry: "If you could ask your mom or dad one question and know you would get an honest answer, what question would you ask?" The responses have been organized into twelve themes, the same themes as in this book. All duplicate questions from the children have been removed. For example, "Am I adopted?" was asked by nine children in the survey. Questions of too specific a nature (example: Is there any chance I could go to Florida State College?) have either been eliminated or altered to be more general (Is there any chance I could go to college?). All questions have been copied verbatim from the original research, including any grammatical errors.

These questions are provided to give parents, counselors, teachers, youth professionals, and others using this book a better understanding of the types of things that are on the minds of preteens. Use them as conversation starters with the preteen in your life.

1. This Clan Is Our Clan: The Extended Family
How long have you lived in this house?
What is my family background?
Where did our family come from?
What are all my blood types in me?
Can you tell me more about my family past?
Do I have any relatives in other states?
Am I related to a famous person?
Can you give me important family information?

When can I go and see my grandma and grandpa?

How old was our oldest grandpa?

What were my great-grandparents like?

What is your maiden name?

Why do we have last names?

How did we get our last name?

How did my great-grandad die?

What is your family like; I've never seen them.

Why don't you know your mom and dad, and why do you have a
bad temper about it?

Why can't I ever see my uncle?

What happened to my aunt?

Do you like our family and what they do?

What would happen and where would I go if you died or we got
taken away from you for some reason?

What does it feel like to lose a close relative (mom, dad, brother, etc.)?

2. Parents Are People, Too: Each Parent as an Individual

How old are you?

When were you born?

Who are you, really?

What are you scared of?

Are you good?

Who was president when you were born?

What was your worst experience growing up?

What was the most complicated thing that happened to you during
your teenage years?

Can you tell me about your childhood?

What did you do when you were a kid?

Were you pressured to do things when you were little?

Were you ever pressured as a child, and by whom?

What was it like in the 70s? Give details.

What were you like as a child in the 70s? A hippy or a normal child?

What was it like when you were my age?

What were you like when you were little? Were you a nice
    person? Were you bad?

What did you look like when you were little?

When you were young, what did you do when you were afraid?

Why were you adopted/taken away from your real parents?

Did you have low self-esteem or high self-esteem when you were my age?

What did you have to do when you were a kid?

When was the last time you were in a hospital and why?

How long did it take you to reach Eagle Scout?

What is your favorite thing to do?

Are you a happy person?

Do you have high self-esteem or low self-esteem?

When was the last time you enjoyed yourself?

How do you feel today?

What are your favorite moments?

What is your deepest darkest secret?

Do you regret anything that you ever did in your life?

Did you ever make any horrible decisions in your life, and if so
    what consequences happened afterwards?

What bad decisions did you make when you were young?

What were the choices you made as a teen to help shape who
    you are today?

What regrets do you have?

If drugs and alcohol are so bad, why do you do them?

How old were you when you started smoking?

If you tell us not to smoke, why do you?

Mom [Dad], could you quit smoking?

Why do you carry around a lighter, but you don't smoke?

Why do you smoke?

Will you ever stop smoking?

When you were my age, what bad things did you do with friends?

What is the worst thing you've ever done?

Did you ever break a rule when you were a kid?

What was the most trouble you have ever gotten into?

Did you ever smoke?

How many illegal things have you done in your life? What were they?

What's the stupidest thing you ever did?

Have you ever tried any kind of drug?

What are your views on drugs, and have you ever done any?

Have you ever experienced drugs? If so, what are they like?

Have you ever gotten in trouble with the law?

Dad, when did you start your growth spurt?

How old were you when you got your first car?

What kind of car did you first get when you got your license?

Have you ever been arrested?

Did you ever get pulled over by a cop?

Have you ever wrecked into another car or a tree?

Have you ever been in a war?

When you were in the [military] did you ever kill a person?

3. How It Began: Parents as a Couple

When was the first time you met?

How did you meet each other?

When did you go on your first date?

What made you fall in love with each other?

Did you ever go out with your new husband in high school, Mom?

How long have you been together?

Did you get close to marrying anyone else?

How did you know you were in love with each other?

Why did you marry my dad when you knew he would hurt you?

When and why did you decide to get married?

How did you feel about Dad when he proposed to you?

Why did you choose my dad [mom] for your husband [wife]?

Why did you get married at such a young age?

Are you glad you married each other?

When you were younger, was Mom [Dad] the first person you
    wanted to marry?

Why did you get married after not having a good first marriage?

Mom, will you ever get married to him?

How did my father die?

If I could go visit my mom, would you allow me to go and
help me get there?

Will I ever see my mom again?

Can I live with my mom?

If I wanted to live with my dad, could I?

Why can't I live with my dad?

Could we move closer to my dad so I could see him more often?

Mom, can I meet my real dad?

Can I work with my dad, Mom? Please!

How come you really don't let me do a lot of stuff with my dad?

When am I going to see my dad?

How come my dad is not here?

What was my daddy like?

Since you are not my real dad, can I call you by your name?

Dad, can I move in with you because my mom hates me?

What went on between you that caused you to separate?

Why did you get divorced?

Did you have an affair?

Why did you have an affair?

What happened in the past with you and Dad before you got a divorce?

Why did you leave my dad?

Why did you marry [my stepfather] and then divorce him?

Have you ever gotten divorced?

Will you ever get divorced?

Who was my dad's first wife, and what's her name?

Can you get back together without fighting?

Why are you almost always fighting about the stupidest things?

How do you feel about each other, because you're divorced?

Why didn't you tell me my dad isn't my real dad?

Did you have anybody else that you loved?

Did you love Dad before he died?

Did you ever love Mom?

Why can't you just leave your boyfriend for us?

Why do you guys fight sometimes?

Why can't you and Dad get along?

Are you sexually active?

Have you been with anyone besides each other, after you were married?

Have you ever looked at another person with lust?

Have you ever thought about getting remarried?

Are you married to somebody that I don't know about?

4. Me, Myself, and I: Your Child's Beginnings

Do I have high or low self-esteem?

Could I be a different kid in school?

Why am I not anything like my mom?

Why aren't I ever happy?

Why do I have asthma?

Am I adopted?

Mom, were you regretful when you had me at 18?

Are you my real mom and dad?

Am I your real kid, and was I born in this state?

What really happened when I was born?

What would you have named me if I was a girl?

What was I like when I was born? Was I a pest, or was I a good child?

What was I like when I was a baby?

Why did you pick my name?

Was there anything wrong with me when I was born?

Mom, did you think you were going to die when I was being born?

Mom, did it hurt when you gave birth?

Mom, how did it feel when you had me?

How happy were you when I was born?

Did you want me to be a boy or girl?

Am I your first child?

Was I an accident?

How come I'm not the oldest?

Why did you decide to have kids?

Did you want to have kids?

Did you want to have me?

Why did you have me?

How old were you when you had me?

Where was I born?

What is the truth about my complicated childhood? Who abused me? Who did I live with?

How was I born?

Do you know where I'll die?

5. Love Me Tender: Support and Conflict Between Parent and Child

Do you love me and would you ever give me up?

How much do you really love me?

If someone told you they would give you $100,000,000,000,000,000 for me, would you give me up to them?

Do you love me as much as the next person?

Why am I important to you?

If I was not your child, would you like me as a person?

What one thing do you honestly hate about me?

What don't you like about me, and what can I do to fix it?

Am I ugly?

Do you think I am good in sports compared to _____?

Do you think I have a chance in the real world?

Honestly, what kind of person do you think I am, and what are my true strengths and weaknesses?

What do you really think of me?

How can I improve as a person?

Do you think I'm a bad kid?

Do you think I'm a good kid?

Do you think I'm important?

Do you think I'm gay?

Do you think I'm handsome or smart, and do you love me?

What do you honestly expect from me as a daughter?

What do you think I'm best at?

Do you think I'm stupid?

Am I really smart?

Would you be really sad if I ran away because you were fighting?

What would you do if I died?

Do you like it when I talk too much?

Do you like my crazy ways?

Can I have a hug?

Can you kiss me?

If I had a baby, would you help me take care of it?

If you found out that I had sex or was pregnant, what would your reaction be?

If I got pregnant, would you honestly kick me out of the house and disown me?

Would you approve of me hanging out and being friends with a pregnant girl or a person who's involved with drugs?

How would you feel to know that I am anorexic and bulimic?

Will you always be with me even when I have my children?

What would you say if I did drugs?

What would happen if I were to do drugs?

If I get in trouble any time, will you tell me so I can correct my mistakes?

Would you hate me if I joined the military?

How come you always think that since I don't talk to you often that means I hate you?

Why do you blame me for everything?

When you get your period, why do you get so mad at me and yell and take everything out on me?

Why are you so mean all the time?

Mom, why do you complain about things not worth the complaining?

Why do you break me down inside and hurt me outside all the time?

Why do you drink, and why do you call me names when you are mad at someone?

Dad, why is my mom most of the time in a grouchy mood?

Would you ever hurt me in any way?

Why do you act the way you do?

Why do you always take my sister's [brother's] side?

How do my social, school, and daily habits negatively affect you?

How come you were never here for me?

Why don't you have any time for me?

Could I go places with you or do something with you?

Can I spend more time with you and my sister?

Can you and I go swimming, or do you want to go to the mall?

Can we have a mother-daughter day?

Why won't you take me anywhere?

Are you coming to my football game?

Why can't I join the family gatherings?

Why don't you ever talk to me about girls?

Why don't you talk to me about drugs or sex?

Why don't parents talk openly with children if we talk openly with them?

Why don't we talk like a real family?

Can we stay together forever?

How much time do we have together until you pass away?

If I have a problem, who can I talk to?

Can I fall back to you if I have a problem?

6. Roots and Wings: Trust and Responsibility Between Parent and Child

How come because I don't tell you what's going on in my life, you
   think I'm doing bad stuff?

Can you totally trust me?

Can I do anything I want?

Why do parents think all that teenagers do is bad, and why don't
   people respect us?

Have you ever gone through my things and read my notes and
   private things?

Have you ever gone through my belongings?

Have you ever lied to me in the past year?

Have you ever had to lie to us?

Can we talk about trust in the family?

Could I have free will?

Why can't I stay home alone?

How come parents think they are always right?

Am I allowed to do whatever I want to?

Why can't I wear what I want to?

Why don't I have the same rights as you?

Why are you so protectful?

Are some of your rules really necessary?

What makes you make the choices you do make when you discipline me?

Why do you think grounding me will change anything?

Could you stop bossing me around?

Why do you treat me like a little girl?

Why are you so strict towards me?

Are you always going to tell me what to do?

Am I old enough to do stuff on my own?

Can I go camping by myself in the woods someday?

Why am I not allowed to swear?

Why do we have responsibility?

Why do we have to do chores every day?

Why don't I make money on average like everyone else?

Do I have to clean my room?

Do I have to do chores or work before I go outside?

Why do I have to do so much work?

Why am I not allowed to go out and have fun?

Am I allowed to ride my bike to the other side of town?

How long am I allowed up, and how long am I allowed outside?

Could I stay up later on Friday nights?

Could I stay out until 10:30 only on weekends, and
     on weekdays 7:30, and get an allowance?

Can I go out and play?

Can I get involved more in sports, clubs, etc.?

Can I go over to my friend's house?

Can I do more with my friends?

Could I go to my friend's house for a week?

Can my friend sleep over?

Can I go to the movies with my friends?

Can I go to a party with my friends?

Can I go to a concert by myself with a friend?

Could I go out on Fridays to get out, have fun, and socialize
more with my friends and others?

Can I go out and not come back until morning?

Am I old enough to have a baby-sitting job?

Why am I not allowed on the phone?

7. Everybody Needs a Friend: Peers and Friendships

Who was your best friend?

Who is your best friend?

How many friends did you have when you were younger?

Were you popular in school?

What does friendship mean to you?

Why do kids judge other kids if they don't even know them?

Why do people hate me?

Could I have a friend come over?

Why doesn't anyone like me?

Why are some people always so mean to me?

Why are my friends always so mean to me?

Why is my friend mad at me and they're not my friend?

How do you get people to like you for a friend?

How do you fit in with a group?

What would you do if someone is bothering you?

Why don't all people keep secrets as good as I do?

What is your opinion on my problems with friends and relationships?

8. What's Love Got to Do with It? Romantic Relationships

Mom, who was your first crush, besides Dad?

What age did you start dating?

How old were you when you had your first boyfriend/girlfriend,
    and who was it?

How many guys have you dated?

At what age did you first kiss someone or have a serious
    relationship with them?

When did you kiss for the first time in your life?

How many girls did you kiss before?

Is it true that you never kissed a boy until you were married?

Did you beat off when you were a kid?

How many times have you had sex?

When was the first time you had sex?

How old were you when you first had sex?

Did you have sex before marriage?

Is sex a good thing or not?

How many people have you had intercourse with?

How old were you when you started looking at nude women?

Dad, how old were you when you felt someone for the first time?

How do you know that you like someone and that he likes you?

Why is it so wrong to like guys as boyfriends?

Can you tell me how to get girls?

When you like a boy, should you tell him or not?

Why do people love?

Why am I not allowed to date?

When can I date and go to boy-girl parties?

Can I have a party with girls and boys?

Could I have a boy-girl sleepover?

When can I go out on my first date?

Could I go on a car date when I'm 14 and my date is 16 or 17?

Why do you have a problem with me dating blacks?

If I am going out with a boy, and my friend comes along
    and starts flirting with him, when they are just really
    good friends . . . Do you think that is wrong?

Would it be okay to dance with someone closely?

Can we talk about relationships?

Can we talk about guys?

Why do people act different around their friends than around their boyfriends or girlfriend?

How old is an appropriate age to get married?

Did you ever think you would never find love?

9. Making the Grade: School

What was it like when you were little kids in school?

Where did you go to school?

What were you like in school?

What kind of grades did you get, and what did Grandma and Grandpa do if you got a bad grade?

How was school when you were a kid?

What activities did you do in school?

What did you do in high school? Did you get in trouble at all?

How old were you when you dropped out of school?

What bad things did you do in school?

Why didn't you go to college?

Why or what encouraged you not to go to college?

How would you feel if I got kicked out of school?

Can you help me with a problem I have in school?

If I would flunk, what would you do? Would you help me or let me flunk again?

Would you be mad at me if I flunked?

Do you think I am doing good in school?

Why do most kids hate school?

Why is it so important to you that I get good grades, stay in school, and don't do drugs?

Why do we have to go to school for twelve grades?

Can we get a new principal?

What day does school end?

Will you help me with my homework?

Can you help me with school and sports?

Does high school bring on a lot of pressure as far as
   drugs and school work?
Can I ask you some things about school?
Can you home school me?

10. Nine to Five: Work

What did you want to do for a job when you were little?
What was your main goal as a child? What did you want to be?
Mom, what did you want to be when you were grown up?
Can we talk about what I want to be when I am an adult?
What should I be when I grow up?
Can you make recommendations for a good college education;
   where to go, etc?
Mother, I want to go to college. Is there a possible way I can go to
   college? Can you support me through it?
Would you be proud if I go to college?
Can we talk about college and my future career?
Will I be going to college?
What do you think would be the best choice for my future?
What are good jobs?
What should I be (i.e., job) to support myself in the future?
What businesses should I work at since I don't have perfect grades?
How long does it take to become a doctor?
When can I be a major league baseball player?
Would an electrician be a good job to go into?
Do you think I'll succeed in life?
Do you truly believe that I can fulfill my dream?
What are the best ways to be successful in my older years?
What do you do with all of our money, really?
How much money do you make?
What is our financial situation?
Where would we go if we lost our home?
Why are you so cheap?
Would you buy a million dollar car?

When is your next check coming in?

What do you do at your job?

What is the best part of your job?

If you could have a different career than you have now, what would it be?

If you could change to any other job, what would you do?

What jobs did you have that you liked most in the past?

Why did you change jobs?

Why did you decide to become a minister?

When are you going to be done flying around the United States?

11. Looking to the Future: Adulthood

What does it feel like to be an adult?

What is it like in the grown-up world?

Were you scared about growing up when you were a kid?

What were your dreams when you were little?

Would you stand by the decisions I make in life?

If I were to become a total failure, would you still praise me
    as if I was successful?

Is life going to be hard or easy for me when I grow up?

What does it feel like to be a grown-up and driving?

Is it fun to be an adult?

Is it hard being an adult?

What is it like to be a parent?

Is it hard raising three kids on your own, or is it an okay job?

What is it like to have kids like me and my sisters?

When we grow up, how hard is it in life to keep up on the bills?

Do you get more respect when you are older?

Where do you want me to be living in 10 years?

12. Is This Just the Way It Is? Life

Will you tell me about life?

What things are important for life?

What is your perspective of life?

What is the most important thing to you?

Are you afraid to die?

Why is there so much killing in the world?

Do you think there will be a World War III?

Do you really care about people you don't like or don't even know?

Do you really get radiation from sitting near the TV?

Why do we have sports in the world?

Why do animals not live as long as people?

When will Jesus come?

Is there really a Santa Claus?

Why do people have to work to get paid and not the government just pay you every week so much money?

What is the point of living?

Why are we on Earth?

Why do people have to die?

Why do kids want to kill other kids, and bomb their school and hurt innocent people?

Why do people act so mean to each other?

Are people usually nicer than they seem?

Why do people love each other?

Why do some people have complications and others don't?

Why do so many people have no respect at all, and why are people so mean to others?

Why do people have bad tempers?

Why do people have to be so violent and mean?

Why are people so rude and inconsiderate?

Why were drugs invented?

Why do people do drugs?

Why do people smoke and drink?

Why do girls have to go through more things than boys do?

Selected Readings and Resources

Benson, P. L., J. Galbraith and P. Espeland. *What Kids Need to Succeed*. Minneapolis, MN: Free Spirit Publishing, 1998

Blaney, Susan. *Please Stop the Rollercoaster: How Parents of Teenagers Can Smooth Out the Ride*. Acton, MA: ChangeWorks Publishing & Consulting, 2004

Currie, Eliott. *The Road to Whatever: Middle-Class Culture and the Crisis of Adolescence*. New York: Metropolitan Books, 2004

Faber, Adele, and Elaine Mazlish. *How to Talk So Kids Will Listen, and Listen So Kids Will Talk*. New York: Avon Books, 1999

——. *How to Talk So Teens Will Listen, and Listen So Teens Will Talk*. New York: Collins, 2006

Fox, Lara, and Hilary Frankel. *Breaking the Code: Two Teens Reveal the Secrets to Better Parent-Child Communication*. New York: Penguin Group, 2005

Gatto, John Taylor. *Dumbing Us Down: The Hidden Curriculum of Compulsory Schooling*. Philadelphia: New Society Publishers, 1992

Giannetti, Charlene C., and Margaret Sagarese. *The Roller-Coaster Years: Raising Your Child Through the Maddening Yet Magical Middle School Years*. New York: Bantam Doubleday Dell, 1997

Gore, Ariel, with Maia Swift. *Whatever, Mom: Hip Mama's Guide to Raising a Teenager*. Emeryville, CA: Seal Press, 2004

Heyman, Richard. *How to Say It to Teens: Talking About the Most Important Topics of Their Lives*. Paramus, NJ: Prentice Hall, 2001

Llewellyn, Grace. *The Teenage Liberation Handbook: How to Quit School and Get a Real Life and Education*. Eugene, OR: Lowry House, 1998

——. *Real Lives: Eleven Teenagers Who Don't Go to School*. Eugene, OR: Lowry House, 1993

Males, Mike. *The Scapegoat Generation: America's War on Adolescents*. Monroe, ME: Common Courage Press, 1996

Packer, Alex J. *Bringing Up Parents: The Teenager's Handbook*. Minneapolis: Free Spirit Press, 1992

Perlstein, Linda. *Not Much Just Chillin': The Hidden Lives of Middle Schoolers*. New York: Farrar, Straus and Giroux, 2003

Richardson, Justin, and Mark Schuster. *Everything You Never Wanted Your Kids to Know About Sex: But Were Afraid They'd Ask*. New York: Three Rivers Press, 2003

Rosenberg, Marshall. *Nonviolent Communication: A Language of Compassion*. Encinitas, CA: Puddledancer Press, 2000

Schaefer, Charles E., and Theresa Foy DiGeronimo. *How to Talk to Teens About Really Important Things*. San Francisco: Jossey-Bass, 1999

Steinberg, Laurence, and Ann Levine. *You and Your Adolescent: A Parent's Guide for Ages 10–20*, Revised Edition. New York: Harper Collins, 1997

Steinberg, Laurence, and Wendy Steinberg. *Crossing Paths: How Your Child's Adolescence Triggers Your Own Crisis*. New York: Simon & Schuster, 1994

Steinberg, Laurence. *Adolescence, Seventh Edition.* New York: McGraw-Hill, 2005

Steinberg, Laurence. *The 10 Basic Principles of Good Parenting.* New York: Simon & Schuster, 2004

Stepp, Laura Sessions. *Our Last Best Shot: Guiding Our Children Through Early Adolescence.* New York: Penguin Putnam, 2000

Thomson, Lenore. *Personality Type: An Owner's Manual.* Boston: Shambhala Publications, 1998

Walsh, David. <u>*Why*</u> *Do They Act That Way?: A Survival Guide to the Adolescent Brain for You and Your Teen.* New York: Simon & Schuster, 2004

Wipfler, Patty. *Supporting Adolescents.* Palo Alto, CA: Hand in Hand Parenting, 2007

Websites

www.familiesaretalking.org
The website of the Sexuality Information and Education Council of the United States (SIECUS), the leading voice in promoting comprehensive sexuality education. The site provides helpful information to parents and to young people about human sexuality.

www.handinhandparenting.org
A website helping parents build and rebuild connection with their children and with other parents to strengthen families and communities.

www.nmsa.org
The website of the National Middle School Association, an organization dedicated to improving the educational experiences of young adolescents. Resources for middle-school teachers, administrators, and parents are available.

www.mediawise.org
The website of the National Institute on Media and the Family, which provides ratings and reviews of videogames, movies, and TV shows.

www.parenting247.org
A website sponsored by the University of Illinois Extension, providing useful information to parents of any age child.

www.pflag.org
The website for PFLAG (Parents, Families and Friends of Lesbians and Gays), which promotes the health and well-being of gay, lesbian, bisexual, and transgender persons and works to end discrimination and secure equal civil rights.

www.pleasestoptherollercoaster.com
The website of Susan Blaney, author of *Please Stop the Rollercoaster*, featuring solutions, tips, and resources for parenting teenagers.

www.talkingwithkids.org
A website to help parents talk to teenagers about tough issues like sex, drugs, violence, alcohol, and HIV/AIDS.

www.youthrights.org
The website for the National Youth Rights Association, a youth-led national nonprofit organization dedicated to fighting for the civil rights and liberties of young people.

Activities Index

adoption, books about, 60

adult, interviewing to learn when one becomes an, 155–156

adulthood, celebrating steps toward, 156

affection, ways to express, 119

alcohol or drugs, reasons not to use, 167

anger, defusing, 167

appreciating what's done right, 88

arguing by appointment, 72

baby book, 59

bad behavior by teen(s), newspaper article on, 87

best day ever, planning with a friend, 105

best friend's qualities, listing, 105

birthday, writing letter for child's eighteenth, 156

Checklist for Adulthood, 156

childhood friends, qualities of parent's, 105

coat of arms, 23

dating: house rules for, 118; reasons to have a boy- or girlfriend, 119; saying "No!" 118–119

donations, making, 167

eulogy, writing for yourself, 167

excuses, best school or work, 35

expenses, discussing regular monthly, 143

family meeting, monthly, 73

family tree, 23

family values, 23

favorite activities, learning more about child's, 88

Ferris Bueller day, planning a, 35

Ferris Bueller's Day Off manifesto, writing a, 35

firsts, looking forward to, 88

friends, things to do with, 119

friendship, starting a, 105

genealogy, 23

Good Times Memory Book, 73

house rules: for dating, 118; in general, 87

I-love-you notes, 72

job, watching someone on the, 143

job salaries and descriptions, 143

jobs for brains and/or muscles, 143

Just Between Us, journal, 72

legal ages, researching, 156

Lend Me Your Ear, box, 73

light shine, ways you can let your, 131

loving each other, silly and serious reasons for, 71

memory lane, walking down, 35

Mom or Dad and Me, monthly day, 71

"No!" 25 ways to tell someone, 118–119

oldest relative: family tree completion with help from, 23; helping label photographs, 23; interviewing, 22–23

partner, thoughts about past choice of, 48

permission, criteria for granting, 88

photo album of child's friends and activities, 104

photos of parent as a baby, 60

pregnancy, talking about teen, 119

quotations, inspirational, about learning or success, 130

Random Acts of Kindness Week, 166

romance terms across the generations, 117

salary, change in parent's, over time, 144

school day off for fun, value of, 35

sex, talking with child about, 119

silver linings, finding, 167

Sputnik event, 144

success in school: 5 things child needs from parent to be a, 131; thank-you notes for caring about, 130; ways to support your preteen's, 131

talents, identification of each other's, 87

teen years of parent, 35

thank-you notes for caring, 130

Things I Know Now . . . About Choosing a Partner, 48

This Is Your Life, party, 48

time capsule: creating with friends, 105; on Internet, 60

timeline of parents' relationship, 47

trips to places in parent's life, 105

two truths and a lie, 48

volunteering, 167

words, learning new, 131

work, bringing son or daughter to, 144

worries of parents, reasons behind the, 88

Book Index

acceptance
    absence of parental, 64–65
    need for, 62
activities (Refer to Activities Index on page
        188.)
addictions. *See* drugs, alcohol, or tobacco
adolescence, changes during
    in parent–child relationship, 61–62
    physical, 1, 54, 107, 110
    social, 1, 90, 93, 106–107
    thinking, 1, 17, 120–121, 145, 158
adoption, 5, 15–16, 50–52, 149
adult, definitions of term, 146
adulthood, 145–149
    milestones toward, 148
    responsibilities in, 147–148
affection, expressing, 61–66
alcohol. *See* drugs, alcohol, or tobacco
anger, parental, 66
argue, how to, 65
arts, working in the, 135
authority, parental, v. child's autonomy,
        74–80

birth stories, 50
body image, 108
bullying, 91, 92

Carnegie Council on Adolescent
        Development, 2
cell phones. *See* technology and preteens
chat rooms. *See* technology and preteens
clothing, 78
college degrees and employment, 135
communication in general
    between parents and children, 3–4,
        10–13, 25, 64
    with teachers, 125
conflicts between parent and child, 61–66,
        75–80, 91–92
couples, parents as, 36–38
cruelty, social, 159–160

crush, first, 107

dating
    house rules for, 118
    saying "No!" 119
    steady, 108–109
    violence, 108
death, 16, 160
disabilities, 6
disasters, natural, 158
discipline, 13
divorce, 37–38
driver's license, 148
dropouts, high-school, 123
drugs, alcohol, or tobacco, 25–26, 27, 28,
        77, 158, 159

early childhood of your preteen, 49–54
education, value of, 121
employment. *See* work
estranged ones, 16
ethnicity, 6, 15
expectations and aspirations, 124–125
extracurricular activities, 125
extravert, 91

Faber, Adele, 4
fads, 77–78
families, types of, 4–5
family history, 15–16, 37
feedback, asking for, 65
foster parents, 5
friends, things to do with, 119
friends and peers, 89–93

gay. *See* homosexuality
gay or lesbian parents, 5, 6
gender
    roles, 92–93, 134
    significance of, in early upbringing,
        53–54
generation gap, 77–78

Golden Rule, 66
grandparents, 14–15
grandparents parenting grandchildren, 53
grief, 160. *See also* death

high-school dropouts, 123
home, leaving, 147
homelessness, 158–159
homeschooling, 121–122
homework, 124–125
homophobic, 79
homosexuality, 79–80, 106–107, 111. *See also* gay or lesbian parents
humility, 13
Hurricane Katrina, 158

"I" messages, 12, 16, 38, 48, 72
independence in adulthood. *See* adulthood
instant messaging. *See* technology and preteens
intergenerational relationships, 14–15
introvert, 91

labor, manual v. mental, 135
leaving home, 147
lesbian. *See* homosexuality
life, in the bigger picture, 157–161
life skills v. academic learning, 122–124
listening, 11–12, 63
Llewellyn, Grace, 4

Mandela, Nelson, 131
mature relationship, qualities of a, 109
maturity. *See* adulthood; mature relationship
Mazlish, Elaine, 4
mental illness, 159
midlife, 75
minimum wage, 136
mitzvahs, 148
money, earning. *See* work
movie club, 10
movie night, 9
movies, criteria for selection of, 5–6
movies, synopses of and cautions about
    Akeelah and the Bee, 126–127
    Back to the Future, 39–40
    Bend It Like Beckham, 80–82
    Ferris Bueller's Day Off, 29–30
    The Man in the Moon, 112–113
    Mrs. Doubtfire, 43–44
    Now and Then, 99–100
    October Sky, 137–138
    Pay It Forward, 161–162
    Real Women Have Curves, 149–150
    Secondhand Lions, 18–19
    Smoke Signals, 66–67
    Stand by Me, 94–95
    Whale Rider, 54–55
Ms. Foundation for Women, 133

na'ii'ees, 148
National Middle School Association, 2

occupational paths, 135–136

Packer, Alex, 4, 75
parents as a couple, 36–38
parents as people, 24–29
peer pressure, 25–26
peer relationships, 89–93
personalities, when different for parent and child, 91–92
poverty, 159
pregnancy, teen, 108
privilege v. responsibility, 78
puberty, 54, 107, 110. *See also* adolescence, changes during

questions kids want to ask
    in Appendix, 170–185
    in listings at starts of chapters, 14, 24, 36, 49, 61, 74, 89, 106, 120, 132, 145, 157
    general references made to types of, 3–4, 8–9, 16, 50, 62, 74–75, 90, 107, 145, 159, 160
quinceañera, 148

relational aggression, 92
relatives, discomfort with certain, 17
research studies, 2, 27
    as basis for this book, 3–4, 170
responsibility v. privilege, 78

role models, parents as, 26–28, 66, 77
romantic relationships, 106–111

safety, 77, 79
salaries and jobs, 136
salary and status, 134–135
same-sex attraction, 106–107. *See also*
        homosexuality
schools, 120–126
    alternative or charter, 122
    home-, 121–122
screen time, limiting, 125
Search Institute, 2
security, 17
self-esteem, 76, 108, 109, 124
self-reliance, 146
sex, talking about, 110–111, 119. *See also*
        sexual behavior
sexual behavior, 38, 77, 108, 110. *See also*
        romantic relationships
sexual orientation, 79–80. *See also*
        homosexuality
single parents, 4–5, 17
smoking. *See* drugs, alcohol, or tobacco
stay-at-home dads, 134

Steinberg, Laurence, 4, 75, 77
stepparents, 5
stereotypes about adolescents, 76–77
suicide, 79
supporting your preteen, 61–66
support system for parent, 10–11

talent, child's own, 76
teachers, communicating with, 125
technology and preteens, 90–91
teen pregnancy, 108
terminology for middle-school children, 5
test scores, and having a boyfriend, 108
tobacco. *See* drugs, alcohol, or tobacco
topics, addressing sensitive, 12, 16–17, 38
touch, as communication, 13
trust and responsibility, 74–80
twelve-step programs, 28

University of Michigan, 27

victims, 160
violence, 108, 159–160

Williamson, Marianne, 131
work, 132–137

About the Authors

Rhonda A. Richardson, PhD is an Associate Professor in the College of Education, Health and Human Services at Kent State University. For over 20 years, she has taught undergraduate and graduate courses on early adolescence and parent-child relationships to current and future youth workers, middle-school teachers, and family services professionals. She graduated magna cum laude from The College of William and Mary with a BA in Psychology; and she holds MS and PhD degrees from Pennsylvania State University in Human Development and Family Studies.

Dr. Richardson is a Certified Family Life Educator, and a member of the National Council on Family Relations and the National Middle School Association. She has published numerous scholarly articles on adolescence and families and co-edited the book *Attachment in Middle Childhood*, published by Guilford Press in 2005. Dr. Richardson resides in Kent, OH with her husband and younger daughter; her older daughter attends college away from home. She can be reached via email at rrichard@kent.edu.

A. Margaret Pevec, MA works as an educator and life coach with parents of teenagers to help smooth out the rough spots, discover common values, and find the fulfillment that comes from deep connection. Since raising her own children through their teen years, she has been passionate about empowering adolescents and also educating people about adultism (the prejudice against and discrimination of young people due to their age).

In addition to life coach training from the Coaches Training Institute, Ms. Pevec holds her MA in Family Life Education and BS in Educational Studies, both from Kent State University. She is also a long-time practitioner of Re-evaluation Counseling and a facilitator of Our Whole Lives, a comprehensive sexuality education curriculum for young people in grades 7–9. Presently living in Boulder, CO, Ms. Pevec is the mother of five children and has one granddaughter. Visit her website at MargaretPevec.com for more information and to get in touch.